# Basic Skills for the
# TOEFL® iBT

Edaan Getzel
Tanya Yaunish

**Compass
Publishing**

*Speaking* 1

# Basic Skills for the TOEFL® iBT 1
## Speaking

Edaan Getzel · Tanya Yaunish

© 2008 Compass Publishing

Project Editor: Liana Robinson
Acquisitions Editor: Emily Page
Content Editor: Michael Jones
Copy Editor: Alice Wrigglesworth
Contributing Writers: Iain Binns, Kayang Gagiano, Moraig Macgillivray, Micah Sedillos
Consultants: Lucy Han, Chanhee Park
Cover/Interior Design: Dammora Inc

email: info@compasspub.com
http://www.compasspub.com


ISBN: 978-1-59966-152-0

10  9  8  7  6  5
10  09

# Contents

Introduction to the TOEFL® iBT ———————————————— 4

Introduction to *Basic Skills for the TOEFL® iBT* ———————— 7

*Basic Skills for the TOEFL® iBT* Speaking Lesson Plan ————— 12

Unit 1   Independent ———————————————————— 15
           Integrated - Announcement and Student Conversation —— 19

Unit 2   Independent ———————————————————— 25
           Integrated - Art Passage and Lecture ————————— 29

Unit 3   Independent ———————————————————— 35
           Integrated - Student Conversation ————————— 39

Unit 4   Independent ———————————————————— 45
           Integrated - Zoology Lecture ——————————— 49

Unit 5   Independent ———————————————————— 55
           Integrated - Announcement and Student Conversation —— 59

Unit 6   Independent ———————————————————— 65
           Integrated - Astronomy Passage and Lecture ————— 69

**Review 1** ———————————————————————— 75

Unit 7   Independent ———————————————————— 81
           Integrated - Student Conversation ————————— 85

Unit 8   Independent ———————————————————— 91
           Integrated - Environment Lecture ————————— 95

Unit 9   Independent ———————————————————— 101
           Integrated - Announcement and Student Conversation —— 105

Unit 10  Independent ———————————————————— 111
           Integrated - Technology Passage and Lecture ————— 115

Unit 11  Independent ———————————————————— 121
           Integrated - Student Conversation ————————— 125

Unit 12  Independent ———————————————————— 131
           Integrated - Music Lecture ——————————— 135

**Review 2** ———————————————————————— 141

**Transcript** —————————————————————— 147
**Answer Key** —————————————————————— 165
**Speaking Feedback and Evaluation Form** ——————— 193

# Introduction to the TOEFL® iBT

## What is the TOEFL® test?

The TOEFL® iBT (Test of English as a Foreign Language Internet-based Test) is designed to assess English proficiency in non-native speakers who want to achieve academic success as well as effective communication. It is not meant to test academic knowledge or computer ability; therefore, questions are always based on material found in the test.

The TOEFL® iBT test is divided into four sections:
- Reading
- Speaking
- Listening
- Writing

## TOEFL® Scores

TOEFL® scores can be used for:
- Admission into university or college where instruction is in English
- Employers or government agencies who need to determine a person's English ability
- English-learning institutes that need to place students in the appropriate level of English instruction

It is estimated that about 4,400 universities and other institutions require a certain TOEFL® test score for admission.

The exact calculation of a TOEFL® test score is complicated and not necessary for the student to understand. However, it is helpful to know that:
- Each section in the Internet-based test is worth 30 points
- The highest possible score on the iBT is 120 points
- Each institution will have its own specific score requirements

✱ It is very important to check with each institution individually to find out what its admission requirements are.

## Registering for the TOEFL® iBT

Students who wish to take the TOEFL® test must get registration information. Registration information can be obtained online at the ETS website. The Internet address is www.ets.org/toefl.

The website provides information such as:
- testing locations
- identification requirements
- registration information
- costs
- other test preparation material
- test center locations

This information will vary depending on the country in which you take the test. Be sure to follow the requirements carefully. If you do not have the proper requirements in order, you may not be able to take the test. Remember that if you register online, you will need to have your credit card information ready.

# Introduction to the Speaking Section of the TOEFL® iBT

The purpose of the speaking section is to evaluate your ability to speak coherently on your opinions and experiences as well as on information that you have read or heard.

The speaking questions fall into two categories: independent and integrated.

The prompts for speaking questions on the TOEFL® iBT can be categorized into three types:

| Question | Time | | | |
|---|---|---|---|---|
| | Reading | Listening | Preparation | Speaking |
| Independent Q1 | --- | --- | 15 seconds | 45 seconds |
| Independent Q2 | | | | |
| Integrated Q3 | 45 seconds | 1-2 minutes | 30 seconds | 60 seconds |
| Integrated Q4 | | | | |
| Integrated Q5 | --- | 1-2 minutes | 30 seconds | 60 seconds |
| Integrated Q6 | | | | |

For the two independent speaking questions, you should draw upon your own experience and knowledge.

For the remaining four speaking questions, you will speak about what you read and/or hear. Your ideas need to be well-organized, and the language you use needs to be accurate enough to be easily understood.

In particular, each question type will require test-takers to organize their ideas and speak toward different goals:

| Question | Type | Materials | Description |
|---|---|---|---|
| 1 | Independent | None | Describe your experience |
| 2 | Independent | None | Give your opinion and explain why you think this |
| 3 | Integrated | Reading | Restate the opinion of the speaker and the examples used |
| | | Conversation | |
| 4 | Integrated | Reading | Explain how the example from the lecture supports/refutes the reading |
| | | Lecture | |
| 5 | Integrated | Conversation | Restate suggestions and tell which you think is better |
| 6 | Integrated | Lecture | Summarize what you heard |

## How Speaking Will Be Scored

ETS graders will score test-takers' responses according to the following scale:

| Score | General Description | Key Points |
|-------|---------------------|------------|
| 4 | The response answers the question or prompt well. The speaker is easy to understand and there are only minor mistakes with grammar or pronunciation. | Fluent speech that is easy to understand and follow, appropriate use of grammar and vocabulary, ideas explained clearly |
| 3 | The response answers the question or prompt, but not all of the ideas are fully developed. The speaker can be understood, but there are some noticeable mistakes in speaking. | At least two (2) of these problems: pronunciation, pace of speech, wrong word choice, limited use of grammar structures, or incorrect grammar |
| 2 | The response gives only a basic or minimal answer to the prompt. Most sentences can be understood, but some effort is required by the listener because speech is not fluent and pronunciation is not accurate. Some ideas are not clearly explained. | At least two (2) of these problems: the speech is choppy (not fluent), there are mistakes in pronunciation, word choice is incorrect, only basic grammar is used, grammar is used poorly, only basic ideas are presented, explanations are absent or limited. |
| 1 | The response is very short, does not show full understanding of the question or prompt, and is hard for the listener to understand. | At least two (2) of these problems: poor pronunciation is used, speech is choppy (not fluent), there are long or frequent pauses, poor grammar use makes ideas difficult to understand, obviously practiced or formulaic expressions are used, there is lots of repetition of expressions in the prompt. |
| 0 | There is no response or the response is not related to the question or prompt. | There is no response to grade, or the response is not related to the question or prompt. |

## Test management

- You will speak into a microphone attached to a headset.
- Before you begin the speaking section, listen to the headset directions. It is very important that your microphone is working and that your voice can be heard clearly. It is also important that you can hear clearly during the listening section.
- Be aware of time constraints. Check the time with the clock shown in the title bar.
- Independent speaking questions come first.
- Note-taking is permitted. Paper will be provided by the test supervisor. These notes can be studied when preparing your response.
- If you miss something that is said in a conversation or lecture, do not panic. Forget about it, and simply keep listening. Even native speakers do not hear everything that is said.
- You must answer each question as it appears. You can NOT return to any questions later.
- Do not leave any question unanswered. You are NOT penalized for guessing an answer.

# Introduction to the *Basic Skills for the TOEFL® iBT* series

**Basic Skills for the TOEFL® iBT is a 3-level, 12-book test preparation series designed for beginning-level students of the TOEFL® iBT.** Over the course of the series, students build on their current vocabulary to include common TOEFL® and academic vocabulary. They are also introduced to the innovative questions types found on the TOEFL® iBT, and are provided with practice of TOEFL® iBT reading, listening, speaking, and writing passages, conversations, lectures, and questions accessible to students of their level.

**Basic Skills for the TOEFL® iBT enables students to build on both their language skills and their knowledge.** The themes of the passages, lectures, and questions cover topics often seen on the TOEFL® iBT. In addition, the independent topics, while taking place in a university setting, are also accessible to and understood by students preparing to enter university. The academic topics are also ones that native speakers study.

**Students accumulate vocabulary over the series.** Vocabulary learned at the beginning of the series will appear in passages and lectures later in the book, level, and series. Each level gets progressively harder. The vocabulary becomes more difficult, the number of vocabulary words to be learned increases, and the passages, conversations, and lectures get longer and increase in level. By the end of the series, students will know all 570 words on the standard Academic Word List (AWL) used by TESOL and have a solid foundation in and understanding of the TOEFL® iBT.

Not only will *Basic Skills for the TOEFL® iBT* start preparing students for the TOEFL® iBT, but it will also give students a well-rounded basis for either further academic study in English or further TOEFL® iBT study.

### Introduction to the *Basic Skills for the TOEFL® iBT* Speaking Book

This is the first speaking book in the *Basic Skills for the TOEFL® iBT* series. Each unit focuses on a different integrated question.

| Units | Integrated Question | Content |
|---|---|---|
| 1, 5, 9 | Q3 | Announcement and student conversation |
| 2, 6, 10 | Q4 | Reading passage and lecture |
| 3, 7, 11 | Q5 | Student conversation |
| 4, 8, 12 | Q6 | Lecture |

Each unit is separated into 7 sections:

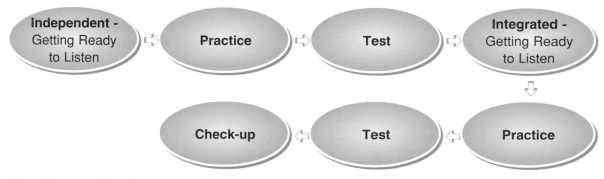

The following will outline the activities and aims of each section.

## Independent - Getting Ready to Listen

### Key Vocabulary and TOEFL® Vocabulary

Students begin by studying the vocabulary they will encounter in the following section. **TOEFL® Vocabulary** includes the words that have been found to appear most often in TOEFL® preparation materials or are Academic Word List (AWL) words. TOEFL® Vocabulary includes the most important words for the student to learn in order to build his or her vocabulary before further TOEFL® study. **Key Vocabulary** includes the other words that are important for the student to know in order to understand the conversation that will follow.

### Prompt

In this part, students are asked some simple questions about an experience in their own lives. This introduces students to the theme of the independent section and gets students talking about things with which they are familiar.

## Practice

### Prompt 1

Students ask each other questions about another experience in their own lives and then make a list of descriptive words that fit in with the prompt and that will be useful later for the test section.

### Prompt 2

Students write answers to another aspect of the independent section's theme and then tell their answers to a partner. They then make another list of descriptive words that will be useful for the test section.

### Prompt 3

Students are now introduced to the main prompt that will also be used in the test section and are given a list of words or phrases that will be useful for the test section.

### Sample Response and Outline

Students will listen to two sample responses to the prompt and will fill out the outlines for them. This will enable students to hear the structure a response should take, and give them ideas for their own response in the test section. They will also get practice on how they can prepare for their own response using an outline. These responses will use all the vocabulary words studied at the beginning of the unit.

### TOEFL® Vocabulary Practice

The next part contains sentences using the TOEFL® vocabulary the student learned at the beginning of the section. This helps students practice the words in context.

## Test

The test contains the same prompt that the students were introduced to in the practice section. They will now have the opportunity to create their own response.

The test is split into three steps and an extension. The first step allows the student to read the prompt as would happen in the real TOEFL® test. The second step then enables the student to prepare his or her response and in the third step students are given the opportunity to write out their responses to make them easier for the teacher to evaluate. The extension activity enables students to then practice responding to the prompt with three partners, and to time one another.

The answer key gives two further responses, which use many of the vocabulary words learned at the beginning of the section.

## Integrated - Getting Ready to Listen

The integrated section varies depending on which TOEFL® question it is focusing on. This section will therefore identify which unit is being described.

### Key Vocabulary and TOEFL® Vocabulary

This contains the Key Vocabulary and TOEFL® Vocabulary students will encounter in the following section. See the independent description for further details.

### Units 1, 2, 5, 6, 9, and 10
### Reading

In these units, students will be asked to read an announcement or reading passage. They are then asked two questions about what they have just read and one question about what they think the conversation/lecture will be about. The aim is to introduce the students to the theme of the integrated section.

### Units 3, 4, 7, 8, 11, and 12
### Listening

In these units, students will be asked to listen to the first part of a conversation or lecture. They are then asked two questions about what they have just heard and one question about what they think the rest of the conversation/lecture will be about. The aim is to introduce the students to the theme of the integrated section.

## Practice

**Units 1, 2, 5, 6, 9, and 10**
Announcement/Reading Passage

Students read the announcement/reading passage again and underline the key information.

### Note-taking

Students now listen to the corresponding conversation or lecture. The reading and listening together contain all the vocabulary words learned at the beginning of the integrated section.

Students take notes as they listen. The notes are guided so that the student can fill in the parts that are missing.

### Prompt

Students are now given the prompt to which they need to respond.

**Units 3, 4, 7, 8, 11, and 12**
Note-taking

Students now listen to the full conversation or lecture. The listening contains all the vocabulary words learned at the beginning of the integrated section.

Students take notes as they listen. The notes are guided so that the student can fill in the parts that are missing.

The student is then asked to answer further questions about the listening. This helps the student prepare for his or her response.

### Prompt

Students are now given the prompt to which they need to respond.

**All Units**
Sample Response and Outline

The students now listen to a sample response and complete the outline for it. This will enable students to hear the structure a response should take and practice how they can prepare for their own response with an outline.

### Speaking Practice

Students should now practice saying a response using the information in the completed outline.

### TOEFL® Vocabulary Practice

The next part contains sentences using the TOEFL® vocabulary the student learned at the beginning of the integrated section. This helps students practice the words in context.

Test

## Units 1, 2, 5, 6, 9, and 10

In these units, the test is split into five steps and an extension. In **step one**, students read the announcement/passage. In **step two**, they listen to the conversation/lecture and complete the notes. In **step three**, they read the prompt. In **step four**, they complete an outline for their response. In **step five**, they write out a full response and in the extension, they practice their response with three partners, and time one another.

## Units 3, 4, 7, 8, 11, and 12

In these units, the test is split into four steps and an extension. In **step one**, students listen to the conversation/lecture and complete the notes. In **step two**, they read the prompt. In **step three**, they complete an outline for their response. In **step four**, they write out a full response and in the extension they practice their response with three partners, and time one another.

Check-up

## Key Vocabulary Practice

This part is sentences using the Key vocabulary the student learned over the course of the unit. This helps students practice the words in context.

# Basic Skills for the TOEFL® iBT

## Sample Speaking Lesson Plan - 50 minutes

| | | |
|---|---|---|
| Homework Check | 5 min. | • Check that students completed their homework and talk about any problems they had. |
| Review | 5 min. | • Review the strategies discussed in the previous unit and talk about other strategies students might have employed when they did homework.<br>• Compare the answers different students gave in their homework and ask some students to speak in front of the class while the rest of the class is split into groups and evaluates them using the form at the back of the book. All students should have to speak in front of the class at least once over the course of the book. |
| Main Lesson | 35 min. | ✱ Students often find the independent sections easier, so these could be completed for homework. The independent and integrated sections may also be alternately taught in the classroom.<br><br>**Integrated - Getting Ready to Speak** (Unit 1 used as an example)<br>A. Learn the words<br>  • Preview the vocabulary and have students read the words aloud.<br>  • Talk about what parts of speech the words belong to.<br>B. Read/Listen<br>  • Have the students read and then answer the questions with a partner.<br>  • As a class, predict what the conversation will be about.<br><br>**Practice**<br>A. Announcement<br>  • Read the announcement again, this time as a class. Try to identify the most important information in it.<br>B. Note-taking<br>  • Have students listening to the conversation and take notes.<br>  • Ask students to compare their notes with a classmate and ensure they all have the main information. Emphasize that each student's notes may be written differently, but that they should all include the same main points.<br>C. Prompt<br>  • Read the prompt as a class and discuss the meaning of it. Ensure that all students have the same understanding of the prompt.<br>D. Sample response and outline<br>  • Put students into groups and play the sample response. You may need to play it two or three times. The group should then have a completed outline.<br>  • Compare each group's outline and ensure that each has the correct information.<br>E. Speaking practice<br>  • Have each student in the group take turns saying the response by following the same completed outline. Emphasize that each response should include the same information but that sentences and vocabulary may differ.<br>F. TOEFL vocabulary practice<br>  • Ask students to complete the sentences and check their answers in pairs.<br><br>**Test**<br>  • Students should complete the test individually.<br>  • Compare outlines and practice the response with a partner. They should evaluate each other using the form at the back of the book.<br><br>**Independent - Getting Ready to Speak** (Next unit)<br>A. Learn the words<br>  • Preview the vocabulary and have students read the words aloud.<br>  • Talk about what parts of speech the words belong to.<br>B. Read the prompt<br>  • Students should read the prompt and answer the related questions with a partner.<br>  • Students could also ask each other further questions related to the prompt.<br>  • Have students listen to the sample and repeat it. |
| Wrap-up | 5 min. | • Give homework (the rest of the independent section.)<br>✱ The Integrated test and the check-up can also be given as homework. |

# Teaching Tips

- It is strongly recommended that the class go through the target vocabulary prior to starting the rest of the unit.

- It is a good idea to have students make their own vocabulary lists on their PCs or in notebooks. Putting the words under thematic categories (categories of subjects) would be an effective way to study the words.

- It is important to emphasize understanding of the main idea of the conversations and lectures. Students often listen without constructing the framework, which could cause them problems understanding the main points and how they relate to the announcement/passage and the prompt.

- The first class should take time to introduce the outline format. Then, when students are asked to use the outlines later, they are familiar and therefore not as intimidating.

- Note-taking practice needs to be done in class with the teacher's assistance in the beginning because not many students are familiar with note-taking. Gradually, have students take notes in groups, pairs, and then individually.

- Timing students' responses is an effective activity. Teachers can give a target length of time and increase it over the course of the book or series.

- Encourage students to do timed-activities even when they do their homework.

- If students have access to recording devices, then it is good practice to record themselves giving their response and listen back to it, noting where they think they could improve and how long their response is.

- Students can use the definitions and synonyms in the vocabulary section when they give their responses.

- Use the test at the end of each unit as a progress check. Students' responses should become more organized and longer as the book and series progresses.

# [ 01 ] Independent

## Getting Ready to Speak

### A. Learn the words.

**Key Vocabulary**

| break | to interrupt something |
|---|---|
| dull | boring |
| thought | idea; something a person thinks |

**TOEFL Vocabulary**

| serious | thoughtful; not making jokes very often |
|---|---|
| academic | educational; scholarly |
| deserve | to earn |
| plus | also |
| contribute | to help out |

### B. Read the prompt. Then answer the questions.

Talk about your daily routine during the week.

1. What time do you wake up in the morning?
   I wake up at _____.

2. What do you do for fun?
   For fun, I _____.

3. What do you do after school?
   After school, I _____.

👥 Now practice the questions and answers with a partner.

🎧 C. Listen and repeat. `Track 1`

# Practice

## Prompt 1

 **A. Read the prompt. Then take turns answering the questions with a partner.**

**Talk about what you do on weekends.**

1. Where do you go?
2. Where do you eat dinner?
3. What is something special that you sometimes do on the weekend?
4. Is there something special that you do every weekend? If so, what?

**B. Make a list of weekend activity words and phrases with your classmates.**

_____

_____

_____

_____

## Prompt 2

**C. Read the prompt. Then complete the answers with your own information.**

**Talk about differences between the weekend and during the week.**

| What? | During the week, I _____. |
| | On the weekend, I _____. |
| What time? | During the week, I go to bed at _____. |
| | On the weekend, I go to bed at _____. |
| Who? | I see _____ during the week, while |
| | I see _____ on the weekend. |

**Now practice your answers with a partner.**

**D. Make a list of weekday activity words and phrases with a partner. List different activities from those listed in part B.**

_____

_____

_____

_____

**E. Read the prompt. Then underline the phrases you could use in your own response.**

> Some people prefer weekends because they don't have school and they get to do other things. Other people prefer weekdays because they like to learn new things at school and they get to see their friends. Which do you prefer? Why?

**Reasons to prefer weekdays or weekends**

- see friends every day
- do different things
- go to bed late
- is more interesting
- is not dull
- can have a break

## Sample Response and Outline

**F. Listen to the sample responses and complete the outlines.** Track 2

### Sample response 1

**Weekdays:** _____ _____ _____

**Weekends:** _____ _____ _____

**What you do:** _____ _____

**What you do:** _____ _____

**What you prefer:** _____

### Sample response 2

**Weekdays:** _____ _____ _____

**Weekends:** _____ _____ _____

**What you do:** _____ _____

**What you do:** _____ _____

**What you prefer:** _____

## TOEFL Vocabulary Practice

**G. Fill in the blanks with the correct words.**

| serious | academic | deserve | plus | contribute |
|---------|----------|---------|------|------------|

1. Circus performers, especially clowns, are never very _____.
2. You should exercise to stay healthy; _____, it is fun.
3. Some people are good at _____ subjects, such as math and science.
4. If you and your friends _____ a little bit of time to cleaning your city, it will look much better.
5. Students who work hard and do well on tests _____ to get good grades.

# Test

## Step 1

Read the prompt.

> Some people prefer weekends because they don't have school and they get to do other things. Other people prefer weekdays because they like to learn new things at school and they get to see their friends. Which do you prefer? Why?

## Step 2

Create an outline for your response.

_____

**Weekdays:**
_____
_____
_____

**Weekends:**
_____
_____
_____

**What you do:**
_____
_____

**What you do:**
_____
_____

**What you prefer:** _____
_____

## Step 3

Write a response using your outline from above.

I prefer _____.
I think that _____
because _____.
On _____
_____.
Some people may prefer _____ but I much prefer _____.

### Extension

**Work with a partner. Take turns saying your response. Then change partners two more times. Time yourselves!**

Your time: _____ seconds

Partner one's time: _____ seconds

Your time: _____ seconds

Partner two's time: _____ seconds

Your time: _____ seconds

Partner three's time: _____ seconds

# Getting Ready to Speak

**A. Learn the words.**

### Key Vocabulary

| | |
|---|---|
| **exam** | an important test |
| **trouble** | difficulty |
| **resume** | to continue a previous activity |

### TOEFL Vocabulary

| | |
|---|---|
| **due to** | because of; as a result of |
| **final** | last |
| **access** | to gain the ability to use |
| **permanent** | not temporary; continuing indefinitely |
| **ordinary** | normal; usual |

**B. Read the announcement. Then answer the questions.**

> ### Change of Library Hours
> Due to exams, the library will be changing its hours. During the final month of classes, students will be able to access it twenty-four hours a day, seven days a week. This will give students more time to prepare for their exams. This change will not be permanent. The ordinary library hours will resume after exams.

1. What will happen?
   The library will _____.

2. Why is the library doing this?
   So that students can _____.

3. What do you think the conversation will be about?
   I think the conversation will be about _____.

**Now practice the questions and answers with a partner.**

**C. Listen and repeat.** `Track 3`

# Practice

**A. Read the announcement again and underline the key information.**

> ## Change of Library Hours
>
> Due to exams, the library will be changing its hours. During the final month of classes, students will be able to access it twenty-four hours a day, seven days a week. This will give students more time to prepare for their exams. This change will not be permanent. The ordinary library hours will resume after exams.

## Note-taking

**B. Listen to the conversation and take notes.** `Track 4`

| Man | Woman |
|---|---|
| • Has an essay to _____ | • First day of _____ |
| | • Final month of classes, so library open |
| • It's fantastic because _____ | _____ |
| _____ | • Library is open _____ |
| • Now has enough _____ | • Always studies at home, so _____ |
| _____ | _____ |
| • Can't study at home as it _____ | |
| _____ | |
| • Does everything at _____ | |
| • Now has _____ | |
| _____ | |
| • Will help _____ | |

## Prompt

**C. Read the prompt.**

> The man expresses his opinion of the announcement made about the library changing its hours. State his opinion and explain the reasons he gives for holding that opinion.

**D. Listen to the sample response and complete the outline.** `Track 5`

The man thinks the change in hours is _____.

  A.  It will give him more time

      **1.**  to finish _____

      **2.**  to study _____

  B.  The man

      **1.**  can't study _____

      **2.**  does everything _____

  C.  He thinks the longer hours _____.

## Speaking Practice

**E. Now work with a partner. Take turns saying your own response using the outline from above.**

Your time: _____ seconds      Your partner's time: _____ seconds

## TOEFL Vocabulary Practice

**F.  Fill in the blanks with the correct words.**

| permanent | ordinary | access | due to | final |
|---|---|---|---|---|

**1.**  The doctor says her illness is _____. She won't get better.

**2.**  A ski trip may be cancelled _____ bad weather.

**3.**  At the end of the year, many students have a _____ exam.

**4.**  I had to work a few extra shifts last week, but this week I'm going back to my _____ schedule.

**5.**  In public places, you often need an account to _____ a computer.

# Test

## Step 1

Read the announcement.

> **Change in Computer Lab Hours**
>
> It has come to our attention that many students are having trouble accessing a computer. Therefore, starting on September 20th, the computer lab will be open longer. It will open at 7 a.m. rather than 9 a.m. It will close at 11 p.m. rather than 10 p.m. This change is due to increased demand. We hope the new hours will solve this problem.

## Step 2

Listen to the conversation and take notes. **Track 6**

| Man | Woman |
| --- | --- |
| • Hears that the university is _____ _____ | • Thinks changing hours won't _____ _____ |
| • Thinks it's _____ | • Need more _____ |
| • Has trouble accessing _____ _____ | • Works there, so will have to _____ _____ |
| • Thinks that would be best but _____ _____ | • Doubts many students _____ |
| • Thinks it's a _____ | • Sounds permanent but they _____ _____ |
| | • Should use _____ _____ |
| | • Then many students could _____ _____ |

## Step 3

Read the prompt.

> The woman expresses her opinion of the announcement made about the computer lab changing its hours. State her opinion and explain the reasons she gives for holding that opinion.

## Step 4

Create an outline for your response.

The woman is _____.

    A. The woman

        **1.** works at the _____

        **2.** will have to _____

    B. She thinks

        **1.** it will not help because _____

        **2.** the university should _____

## Step 5

Write a response using your outline from above.

> The woman is _____.
> She works at the computer lab, so _____.
> She thinks _____ because
> most students _____.
> Therefore, instead of paying workers more, the university should _____
> _____.

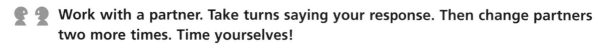 **Work with a partner. Take turns saying your response. Then change partners two more times. Time yourselves!**

Your time: _____ seconds      Partner one's time: _____ seconds

Your time: _____ seconds      Partner two's time: _____ seconds

Your time: _____ seconds      Partner three's time: _____ seconds

# Check-up

**Fill in the blanks with the correct words.**

| resume | exam | trouble | break | dull | thoughts |
|--------|------|---------|-------|------|----------|

1. Studying hard will prevent _____ on your test later.

2. Classes often _____ in January after a two-week break for the winter holidays.

3. You must do well on your final _____ to advance to the next grade.

4. The soccer player, Pelé, was so famous that two armies at war in Africa took a _____ so they could meet him.

5. Every person has his or her own _____ on how their President should run the country.

6. _____ speeches can make people fall asleep.

# [ 02 ] Independent

## Getting Ready to Speak

### A. Learn the words.

**Key Vocabulary**

| | |
|---|---|
| **pastime** | a hobby; a diversion |
| **interesting** | attention-getting; arousing a feeling of interest |
| **outgoing** | friendly |

**TOEFL Vocabulary**

| | |
|---|---|
| **opposite** | different in every way; the reverse |
| **personality** | the qualities that make people different |
| **different** | not alike or the same |
| **activity** | something that you do |
| **similar** | almost the same but not exactly; like |

### B. Read the prompt. Then answer the questions.

Talk about your best friend.

1. What is your best friend's name?
   My best friend's name is _____.

2. When did you meet your best friend?
   I met my best friend _____.

3. What do you and your best friend like to do?
   We like to _____.

**Now practice the questions and answers with a partner.**

**C. Listen and repeat.** Track 7

# Practice

Prompt 1

**A. Read the prompt. Then take turns answering the questions with a partner.**

Talk about your best friend's and your personalities.

1. What is your personality?
2. What is your friend's personality?
3. Are your personalities similar or very different?
4. Do you think this is good or bad? Why?

**B. Make a list of personality words and phrases with your classmates.**

_____

_____

_____

_____

Prompt 2

**C. Read the prompt. Then complete the answers with your own information.**

Talk about pastimes that you and your friends enjoy.

| | |
|---|---|
| What? | One pastime that I enjoy doing with my friends is _____. |
| Where? | We often go to _____. |
| When? | Usually, we _____. |
| Why? | I like my friends because _____. |

**Now practice your answers with a partner.**

**D. Make a list of hobbies with a partner.**

_____

_____

_____

_____

**E. Read the prompt. Then underline the phrases you could use in your own response.**

> Some people think best friends usually have similar personalities and like the same things. Others think best friends usually have opposite personalities and like different things. What do you think?

**Reasons for being friends**

- share feelings
- help each other
- learn from each other
- share experiences
- have fun together
- have the same goals

## Sample Response and Outline

**F. Listen to the sample responses and complete the outlines.** `Track 8`

### Sample response 1

⬭ _____

**My personality:**     **My friend's personality:**

_____     _____
_____     _____

**Like to do:**

_____     _____
_____     _____

**Best friends because:** _____
_____
_____

### Sample response 2

⬭ _____

**My personality:**     **My friend's personality:**

_____     _____
_____     _____

**Like to do:**

_____     _____
_____     _____

**Best friends because:** _____
_____
_____

## TOEFL Vocabulary Practice

**G. Fill in the blanks with the correct words.**

| opposite | different | activity | similar | personality |
|---|---|---|---|---|

1. My father and mother are talkative. They have the same _____.
2. The _____ of shy is outgoing.
3. They are both tall and have dark hair. They look _____.
4. Scuba diving is an interesting _____.
5. Candy and fruit are _____ types of food.

# Test

## Step 1

Read the prompt.

> Some people think best friends usually have similar personalities and like the same things. Others think best friends usually have opposite personalities and like different things. What do you think?

## Step 2

Create an outline for your response.

_____

**My personality:**

_____

_____

**Like to do:**

_____

_____

**My friend's personality:**

_____

_____

_____

**Best friends because:** _____

_____

## Step 3

Write a response using your outline from above.

I think that best friends usually have _____.
A good example is me and my best friend. I am _____
and my best friend is _____.
We like to _____
_____.
We are best friends because _____.

### Extension

**Work with a partner. Take turns saying your response. Then change partners two more times. Time yourselves!**

Your time: _____ seconds        Partner one's time: _____ seconds

Your time: _____ seconds        Partner two's time: _____ seconds

Your time: _____ seconds        Partner three's time: _____ seconds

# Integrated

## Getting Ready to Speak

### A. Learn the words.

#### Key Vocabulary

| | |
|---|---|
| outdoor | opposite of indoor; not inside |
| studio | an artist's work space |
| speed | quick movement |

#### TOEFL Vocabulary

| | |
|---|---|
| medium | the way that something is done or the things used to do it |
| nature | the outside world |
| influence | affect someone's behavior |
| realistic | looking real; similar to real life |
| critic | a person who judges or evaluates |

### B. Read the passage. Then answer the questions.

> **Impressionism**
>
> Impressionism is a style of art that was popular in the 1800s. It started in France. The medium was paint on canvas. Impressionists tried to paint their own experiences. Nature and the outdoors influenced them. They mostly painted trees and lakes. They worked outdoors, not in a studio. Speed was important because realistic work had to be finished quickly. Critics did not like this style at first.

1. When was Impressionism popular and where was it started?
   Impressionism was popular in _____ and it was started in _____.

2. What did Impressionists paint?
   Impressionists painted _____.

3. What do you think the lecture will be about?
   I think the lecture will be about _____.

**Now practice the questions and answers with a partner.**

C. Listen and repeat. Track 9

# Practice

**A. Read the passage again and underline the key information.**

> ### Impressionism
> Impressionism is a style of art that was popular in the 1800s. It started in France. The medium was paint on canvas. Impressionists tried to paint their own experiences. Nature and the outdoors influenced them. They mostly painted trees and lakes. They worked outdoors, not in a studio. Speed was important because realistic work had to be finished quickly. Critics did not like this style at first.

## Note-taking

**B. Listen to the lecture and take notes.** `Track 10`

**Impressionists**
- They painted things to _____
- Nineteenth century art supplies were _____

**Nature**
- Artists painted _____
- Monet
  - painted in a _____
  - liked painting _____
  - did not have a real _____
- Nature often _____
- Speed was _____

**Colors**
- Monet tried _____
- Red, yellow, and green for _____
- Cloudy scenes used _____

## Prompt

**C. Read the prompt.**

> The professor and the passage give details about Impressionism. Explain how Monet's style of painting was typical of Impressionists.

**D. Listen to the sample response and complete the outline.** `Track 11`

The lecture and passage were about _____.

A. Impressionists liked to paint

　　**1.** things in _____

　　**2.** while _____

B. Monet

　　**1.** liked to _____

　　**2.** painted in _____

　　**3.** didn't have _____

C. Monet and other Impressionists

　　**1.** painted _____

　　**2.** used different _____

Everything Monet did was _____.

## Speaking Practice

**E. Now work with a partner. Take turns saying your own response using the outline from above.**

Your time: _____ seconds　　　Your partner's time: _____ seconds

## TOEFL Vocabulary Practice

**F. Fill in the blanks with the correct words.**

| nature | realistic | influence | medium | critics |
|--------|-----------|-----------|--------|---------|

**1.** Computers have made it possible to add very _____ effects to movies.

**2.** People who love reading new books sometimes become book _____.

**3.** Who has been the biggest _____ in your life?

**4.** People who like camping often enjoy spending time in _____.

**5.** Vincent van Gogh's _____ was oil paint on canvas.

# Test

## Step 1

Read the passage.

### Berthe Morisot

Berthe Morisot was an Impressionist painter. She was born in 1841. Her parents wanted her to draw or paint. They built a studio for her in their garden. She was friends with other artists like Renoir and Degas. They influenced Morisot. She once modeled for Manet. In 1874, she married his brother.

## Step 2

Listen to the lecture and take notes. **Track 12**

**Berthe Morisot**

- She studied _____
- She began drawing and _____
- Her parents were _____
- Her sisters were _____

**Berthe Morisot's style**

- It was _____
- She used light _____
- It was _____

**Berthe Morisot's paintings**

- She painted _____
- She liked to paint _____
- She didn't like _____

**Berthe Morisot**

- She died in _____

## Step 3

Read the prompt.

The professor and the passage talk about Berthe Morisot. Explain why Morisot became an artist and what her paintings are like.

## Step 4

Create an outline for your response.

The passage and lecture were about _____.

    A. Morisot

        **1.** was born _____

        **2.** started painting and drawing when _____

    B. Her parents were _____

    C. Her sisters were _____

    D. Renoir and Degas influenced _____

    E. Morisot's style was _____

    F. Morisot liked to paint people, _____

## Step 5

Write a response using your outline from above.

> The passage and lecture were about _____.
> She was born in _____. She started painting and drawing _____.
> Her parents were _____
> _____.
> Also, artists like Renoir and Degas _____.
> Her style was _____.
> She liked to paint _____
> _____.

**Extension**

**Work with a partner. Take turns saying your response. Then change partners two more times. Time yourselves!**

Your time: _____ seconds      Partner one's time: _____ seconds

Your time: _____ seconds      Partner two's time: _____ seconds

Your time: _____ seconds      Partner three's time: _____ seconds

# Check-up

**Fill in the blanks with the correct words.**

| speed | outgoing | studio | outdoors | pastime | interesting |
|-------|----------|--------|----------|---------|-------------|

1. Many artists prefer to work in a large _____.
2. Soccer can be played indoors or _____.
3. _____ is very important in car racing.
4. Many people find watching movies _____.
5. A common _____ is watching TV.
6. My sister has many friends. She is very _____.

# [ 03 ] Independent

## Getting Ready to Speak

### A. Learn the words.

**Key Vocabulary**

| | |
|---|---|
| old fashioned | old style; traditional |
| reception | quality of signal received through a radio, television, or phone |
| conversation | discussion; talking |

**TOEFL Vocabulary**

| | |
|---|---|
| technology | machines and systems |
| complicated | difficult to understand |
| dependable | able to be trusted |
| multiple | many |
| custom | a habit or a way that things have been done for a long time |

### B. Read the prompt. Then answer the questions.

Talk about how you use the phone.

**1.** Do you use a cell phone or a regular phone to make your calls?

I use a _____.

**2.** How often do you use your cell phone?

I use it _____.

**3.** Do you like to send text messages?

I _____ to send text messages.

**Now practice the questions and answers with a partner.**

**C. Listen and repeat.** Track 13

# Practice

Prompt 1

👤👤 **A. Read the prompt. Then take turns answering the questions with a partner.**

Talk about how you communicate on the computer.

1. Whom do you send emails to?
2. Do you have a blog? What do you do with your blog?
3. What do you look at on your friends' web pages?
4. Do you like using instant messaging? Why?

**B. Make a list of things that are put on web pages with your classmates.**

_____

_____

_____

_____

Prompt 2

**C. Read the prompt. Then complete the answers with your own information.**

Talk about writing letters.

| | |
|---|---|
| How often? | I write letters _____. |
| Who? | I write letters to _____. |
| Why? | I send letters because _____. |
| What? | I _____ to send letters because _____. |

👤👤 **Now practice your answers with a partner.**

**D. Make a list of communication-related words and phrases with a partner.**

_____

_____

_____

_____

**E. Read the prompt. Then underline the phrases you could use in your own response.**

Technology has changed the way many people communicate. Some people prefer to send emails, write messages on blogs, or use instant messaging. Other people prefer to call on the telephone or write letters. How do you prefer to communicate? Why?

**Phrases for discussing communication**

- impersonal
- everyone can do it
- easy
- send files
- multiple conversations
- online chatting

## Sample Response and Outline

**F. Listen to the sample responses and complete the outlines.** Track 14

| Sample response 1 | | Sample response 2 | |
|---|---|---|---|
| _____ | | _____ | |
| **First reason:** | **Second reason:** | **First reason:** | **Second reason:** |
| _____ | _____ | _____ | _____ |
| _____ | _____ | _____ | _____ |
| **Explain why:** | _____ | **Explain why:** | _____ |
| _____ | | _____ | _____ |
| _____ | _____ | _____ | _____ |
| **Think that:** _____ | | **Think that:** _____ | |
| _____ | | _____ | |

## TOEFL Vocabulary Practice

**G. Fill in the blanks with the correct words.**

| technology | complicated | dependable | multiple | custom |
|---|---|---|---|---|

1. Engines in modern cars are much more _____ than those in older cars.
2. Taking your shoes off when you enter a home is the _____ in much of Asia.
3. _____ has made travel planning much easier.
4. Gambling is not a _____ way to earn money.
5. Good taxi drivers have _____ routes to get where they need to go.

# Test

## Step 1

Read the prompt.

> Technology has changed the way many people communicate. Some people prefer to send emails, write messages on blogs, or use instant messaging. Other people prefer to call on the telephone or write letters. How do you prefer to communicate? Why?

## Step 2

Create an outline for your response.

_____

**First reason:**

_____

_____

**Second reason:**

_____

_____

**Like because:** _____

_____

**Think that:** _____

_____

## Step 3

Write a response using your outline from above.

I like to communicate by _____.
It is great because _____.
In addition, _____.
I can _____.
It is much easier _____.
For me, _____.

### Extension

**Work with a partner. Take turns saying your response. Then change partners two more times. Time yourselves!**

Your time: _____ seconds       Partner one's time: _____ seconds

Your time: _____ seconds       Partner two's time: _____ seconds

Your time: _____ seconds       Partner three's time: _____ seconds

# Integrated

# Getting Ready to Speak

## A. Learn the words.

### Key Vocabulary

| | |
|---|---|
| move away | to go to another place |
| cheap | inexpensive |
| freedom | liberty; the state of being free |

### TOEFL Vocabulary

| | |
|---|---|
| motivated | wanting or ready to do something |
| independent | free to make one's own decisions |
| flexible | adaptable |
| responsible | answerable; accountable |
| immediately | without delay; right away |

## B. Listen to the first part of a conversation. Then answer the questions. Track 15

1. What are the students discussing?
   The students are discussing _____.

2. What reasons does the student give for staying at home?
   The student _____.

3. What do you think the rest of the conversation will be about?
   I think the rest of the conversation will be about _____

   _____.

4. What do you think the student should do?
   I think the student should _____

   _____.

## Now practice the questions and answers with a partner.

## C. Listen and repeat. Track 16

# Practice

**A. Listen to the full conversation and take notes.** [Track 17]

| Reasons to stay home | Reasons to move away |
|---|---|
| • Cheaper because _____ _____ <br> • Wouldn't have to _____ <br> • Knows _____ <br> • Has a lot of _____ <br> • See _____ | • See _____ <br> • Meet _____ <br> • Become _____ <br> • Have _____ <br> • Do _____ |

**B. Use your notes to complete the answers.**

**1.** What are some reasons the students discuss for staying at home?

The students discuss _____
_____.

**2.** What are some reasons the student wants to move away?

The student wants to move away because _____
_____.

**Now practice the questions and answers with a partner.**

**C. Read the prompt.**

> The students discuss living at home and moving away from home. Describe the advantages of each choice. Then state which you think is the better option.

**D. Listen to the sample response and complete the outline.** `Track 18`

The conversation is about _____.

A. Advantages of living at home

    **1.** It's cheaper because she could live _____

    **2.** She knows the city well and _____

    **3.** She wouldn't have to fly home for _____

B. Advantages of living away

    **1.** See a new city and _____

    **2.** Become more independent, so _____

Conclusion: I think _____.

**E. Write your own conclusion using the outline from above.**

Conclusion: I think _____

because _____.

**F. Now work with a partner. Take turns saying your own response using the outline from above.**

Your time: _____ seconds      Partner's time: _____ seconds

**G. Fill in the blanks with the correct words.**

| motivated | decide | flexible | immediately | independent |
|---|---|---|---|---|

**1.** You must _____ what you want to order.

**2.** The more _____ you are, the more successful you will be.

**3.** Please finish this _____ and give it to me.

**4.** Living alone has made me _____.

**5.** My teacher is not _____ about assignment due dates.

# Test

## Step 1

🎧 **Listen to the conversation and take notes.** `Track 19`

| Woman | Man |
|---|---|
| • Thinking of _____ _____ <br> • Needs _____ <br> • Will need to decide if _____ _____ | • The course _____ <br> • Have to be _____ <br> • Make a _____ <br> • Also have to solve _____ <br> • For an online course _____ _____ <br> • It's _____ <br> • Have _____ <br> • It's _____ <br> • An online degree is _____ _____ |

## Step 2

**Read the prompt.**

> The students are discussing online courses. Describe the advantages and disadvantages of taking an online course. Then state if you would like to take one and why.

## Step 3

**Create an outline for your response.**

The conversation is about _____.

    A. Student must

        **1.** be _____

        **2.** make _____

        **3.** solve _____

    B. Online you have to _____

    C. Benefits

        **1.** It's _____

        **2.** You have more _____

        **3.** It's _____

Conclusion: I would prefer _____.

## Step 4

Write a response using your outline.

> The conversation is about _____.
> The student must _____.
> One problem with on-line courses is _____.
> Some advantages of on-line courses are _____
> _____.
> I would prefer _____
> _____.

**Work with a partner. Take turns saying your response. Then change partners two more times. Time yourselves!**

Your time: _____ seconds        Partner one's time: _____ seconds

Your time: _____ seconds        Partner two's time: _____ seconds

Your time: _____ seconds        Partner three's time: _____ seconds

# Check-up

**Fill in the blanks with the correct words.**

| freedom | cheap | move away | old-fashioned | reception | conversations |

1. I don't want to _____ from my friends.
2. Wind power is a _____ form of energy.
3. _____ is an important human right.
4. Most cell phones don't get _____ in elevators.
5. Grandmothers usually wear _____ clothing.
6. Many _____ between presidents are kept secret.

# [ 04 ] Independent

# Getting Ready to Speak

## A. Learn the words.

### Key Vocabulary

| | |
|---|---|
| unlike | not like; different |
| countryside | area outside the city; rural area; farm or wild land |
| air | a layer of natural gases that surrounds the Earth |

### TOEFL Vocabulary

| | |
|---|---|
| advantage | benefit |
| include | to contain |
| moreover | furthermore; besides |
| convenient | making life easier |
| disadvantage | negative quality; unfavorable condition |

## B. Read the prompt. Then answer the questions.

### Talk about your house.

**1.** What kind of house do you live in?
I live in a/an _____.

**2.** What is close to your house?
Near my house there is/are _____.

**3.** What is the best thing about your home?
The best thing about my home is _____.

👤👤 **Now practice the questions and answers with a partner.**

🎧 **C. Listen and repeat.** `Track 20`

# Practice

Prompt 1

**A. Read the prompt. Then take turns answering the questions with a partner.**

Talk about the advantages and disadvantages of living in the countryside.

1. What can you do in the countryside?
2. What do you like most about the countryside?
3. What does the countryside have that the city doesn't have?
4. Is living in the countryside good or bad? Why?

**B. Make a list of words and phrases related to the countryside with your classmates.**

_____

_____

_____

_____

Prompt 2

**C. Read the prompt. Then complete the answers with your own information.**

Talk about the advantages and disadvantages of living in the city.

| | |
|---|---|
| What? | Houses in the city are usually _____. |
| Where? | In the city, there is a lot of _____. |
| When? | At night, children must _____. |
| Why? | Living in the city can be bad because _____. |

**Now practice your answers with a partner.**

**D. Make a list of words and phrases related to the city with a partner.**

_____

_____

_____

_____

**E. Read the prompt. Then underline the phrases you could use in your own response.**

Some people think that living in the countryside is better because it is safer and healthier. Others think that living in the city is better because there are more things to do and because you meet different types of people. What is your opinion?

**Reasons for living in the city or the countryside**
- difficult to get around
- not much space for families
- very safe
- lots of jobs
- much cleaner
- better schools

## Sample Response and Outline

**F. Listen to the sample responses and complete the outlines.** Track 21

**Sample response 1**

It is:
_____
_____
_____

It is:
_____
_____
_____

It has:
_____
_____

Think that: _____
_____

**Sample response 2**

It is:
_____
_____
_____

It is:
_____
_____
_____

It has:
_____
_____

Think that: _____
_____

## TOEFL Vocabulary Practice

**G. Fill in the blanks with the correct words.**

| advantages | include | moreover | convenient | disadvantage |
| --- | --- | --- | --- | --- |

1. One _____ of owning a large car is the high cost of gas.
2. Usually cell phone companies _____ a battery with a new phone.
3. There are many _____ to being able to speak another language.
4. MP3 players are more _____ than cassette players because they are very small.
5. Monkeys are really strong. _____, they are also excellent climbers.

# Test

## Step 1

Read the prompt.

> Some people think that living in the countryside is better because it is safer and healthier. Others think that living in the city is better because there are more things to do and because you meet different types of people. What is your opinion?

## Step 2

Create an outline for your response.

**It is:**

_____
_____
_____
_____

**It has:** _____

**Think that:** _____
_____

**You can:**

_____
_____
_____
_____
_____

## Step 3

Write a response using your outline from above.

I think that living in the _____ has more advantages
than living in the _____.
The city has _____.
The countryside, unlike the city, has _____.
_____ is good because _____.
Moreover, the _____.
Living in the _____ is better because _____.

**Work with a partner. Take turns saying your response. Then change partners two more times. Time yourselves!**

Your time: _____ seconds     Partner one's time: _____ seconds
Your time: _____ seconds     Partner two's time: _____ seconds
Your time: _____ seconds     Partner three's time: _____ seconds

48 | Speaking |

# Integrated

## Getting Ready to Speak

### A. Learn the words.

| Key Vocabulary | |
| --- | --- |
| Arctic | northern polar region, near the North Pole |
| tundra | an area between the icecap and tree line of the Arctic |
| tusk | a long, pointed tooth |

| TOEFL Vocabulary | |
| --- | --- |
| dwelling | living in a particular place |
| herd | a group of animals living together |
| migrate | to go from one place to another |
| adapt | to change with different conditions |
| enemy | an unfriendly opponent; a rival |

### B. Listen to the first part of a lecture. Then answer the questions. Track 22

1. What is the lecture mainly about?
   The lecture is about _____.

2. What is the most famous Arctic animal?
   The most famous Arctic animal is _____.

3. What else do you think the professor will talk about?
   I think the professor will talk about _____.

### Now practice the questions and answers with a partner.

### C. Listen and repeat. Track 23

# Practice

**A. Listen to the full lecture and take notes.** Track 24

- Many Arctic animals
- They live on _____
- Land animals: _____
- A caribou is _____
- A hare is _____
- Sea animals: _____
- The male narwhal has _____
- Sea _____
- Some migrate south _____

**B. Use your notes to complete the answers.**

1. What examples of land-dwelling Arctic animals does the professor talk about?
   The professor talks about _____
   _____.

2. What other examples of Arctic animals does the professor give?
   The professor gives _____
   _____ as examples of other Arctic animals.

**Now practice the questions and answers with a partner.**

**C. Read the prompt.**

The professor talked about different Arctic animals. Using points and examples from the lecture, describe these animals.

**D. Listen to the sample response and complete the outline.** `Track 25`

The lecture is about _____.

A. Land animals

    **1.** Polar bears: _____

    **2.** Caribou: _____

       • Its babies can _____

    **3.** Arctic hares: _____

       • Lives in _____

B. Sea animals such as _____

C. Birds

    **1.** Some stay in _____

    **2.** Some migrate _____

Conclusion: Arctic animals _____

_____.

## Speaking Practice

**E. Now work with a partner. Take turns saying your own response using the outline from above.**

Your time: _____ seconds      Your partner's time: _____ seconds

## TOEFL Vocabulary Practice

**F. Fill in the blanks with the correct words.**

| adapt | dwelling | enemies | herds | migrate |
|-------|----------|---------|-------|---------|

**1.** Dogs and cats are natural _____.

**2.** Buffalo live in small _____.

**3.** Animals have to _____ to changes in their environment.

**4.** Many birds and insects _____ with the changing seasons.

**5.** A fish is a water-_____ animal.

# Test

## Step 1

Listen to the lecture and take notes. **Track 26**

- Polar animals are special
- They have to _____
- Caribou and musk oxen eat _____
- Foxes and wolves eat _____
- Caribou migrate _____
- Musk oxen have _____
- Polar bears and whales have a _____
- Some animals change _____
- Arctic birds change from _____ in summer
  to _____

## Step 2

Read the prompt.

> The professor describes how polar animals adapt to the Arctic. Using points and examples from the lecture, describe the ways that polar animals adapt.

## Step 3

Create an outline for your response.

The lecture is about how polar animals live in the Arctic.

    A. Food

        **1.** Caribou and musk oxen eat _____

        **2.** Foxes and wolves eat _____

    B. Protection from the cold

        **1.** Caribou _____

        **2.** Musk oxen _____

        **3.** Polar bears and whales _____

    C. Protection from enemies _____

The lecture is about how polar animals live in the Arctic.

Conclusion: Arctic animals have adapted well to their environment.

**52** | Speaking |

## Step 4

Write a response using your outline.

> The lecture is about _____.
> Arctic animals eat food that is easy to find. For example, _____
> _____.
> Arctic animals keep warm by _____
> _____.
> Arctic animals can hide because _____.
> They have adapted _____.

**Work with a partner. Take turns saying your response. Then change partners two more times. Time yourselves!**

Your time: _____ seconds     Partner one's time: _____ seconds
Your time: _____ seconds     Partner two's time: _____ seconds
Your time: _____ seconds     Partner three's time: _____ seconds

# Check-up

**Fill in the blanks with the correct words.**

| Arctic | tundra | tusks | unlike | countryside | air |
|---|---|---|---|---|---|

1. Male elephants have two long _____.

2. The _____ is in the far north.

3. There are no trees on the _____.

4. Farms are usually located in the _____.

5. _____ Cuba, Russia is a very large country.

6. A person can die if he or she is unable to breathe in any _____.

# [ 05 ] Independent

## Getting Ready to Speak

### A. Learn the words.

**Key Vocabulary**

| | |
|---|---|
| athletic | active; muscular and strong |
| energize | to make or become active |
| focus | to concentrate |

**TOEFL Vocabulary**

| | |
|---|---|
| physical | needing bodily strength |
| participate | to take part in something |
| socialize | to be a part of a social activity |
| nonphysical | not involving movement of the body |
| connect | to relate to someone or something |

### B. Read the prompt. Then answer the questions.

Talk about your favorite sport.

**1.** What sport is your favorite to play?
My favorite sport to play is _____.

**2.** Why is this your favorite sport to play?
It is my favorite sport to play because _____.

**3.** What is your favorite sport to watch on TV?
My favorite sport to watch is _____.

👤👤 **Now practice the questions and answers with a partner.**

🎧 C. **Listen and repeat.** [Track 27]

# Practice

Prompt 1

👤👤 **A. Read the prompt. Then take turns answering the questions with a partner.**

> **Talk about when you do activities outside.**

1. Whom do you go with?
2. What do you do?
3. Where do you go?
4. How do you feel when you are finished?

**B. Make a list of outside activity words and phrases with your classmates.**

_____

_____

_____

_____

Prompt 2

**C. Read the prompt. Then complete the answers with your own information.**

> **Talk about your favorite things to do inside.**

What?        I like to _____.
Who?         I do this _____.
How often?   I _____.
Why?         I like to _____ because _____.

👤👤 **Now practice your answers with a partner.**

**D. Make a list of indoor activity words and phrases with a partner.**

_____

_____

_____

_____

**E. Read the prompt. Then underline the phrases you could use in your own response.**

> Some people like physical activities such as playing sports. Other people like nonphysical activities, such as watching TV or reading books. What do you prefer? Why?

**Reasons to prefer physical or nonphysical activities**

- getting healthy
- relaxing
- getting hurt
- it is challenging
- get a suntan or sunburn
- it is entertaining

## Sample Response and Outline

**F. Listen to the sample responses and complete the outlines.** Track 28

| Sample response 1 | | Sample response 2 | |
|---|---|---|---|
| First reason: | Second reason: | First reason: | Second reason: |
| _____ | _____ | _____ | _____ |
| _____ | _____ | _____ | _____ |
| _____ | _____ | _____ | _____ |
| Like because: | | Like because: | |
| _____ | _____ | _____ | _____ |
| _____ | _____ | _____ | _____ |
| Think that: _____ | | Think that: _____ | |

## TOEFL Vocabulary Practice

**G. Fill in the blanks with the correct words.**

| physical | nonphysical | participate | socializing | connects |
|---|---|---|---|---|

1. Many high school students spend a lot of their free time _____ with their friends.
2. Climbing to the top of Mt. Everest is an extraordinary _____ accomplishment.
3. In a good movie, the audience always _____ with the story.
4. It is important to _____ in class if you want to understand things better.
5. Reading is a good example of a _____ activity.

# Test

## Step 1

Read the prompt.

> Some people like physical activities such as playing sports. Other people like nonphysical activities, such as watching TV or reading books. What do you prefer? Why?

## Step 2

Create an outline for your response.

**You can:**       **You can:**

_____   _____

_____   _____

_____   _____

_____   _____

**Like because:** _____

_____

**Think that:** _____

_____

## Step 3

Write a response using your outline from above.

I prefer _____.
I like this because _____
_____.
In addition, it allows me to _____.
This is good because _____.
I like _____ because _____.

**Extension**

👤👤 **Work with a partner. Take turns saying your response. Then change partners two more times. Time yourselves!**

Your time: _____ seconds    Partner one's time: _____ seconds

Your time: _____ seconds    Partner two's time: _____ seconds

Your time: _____ seconds    Partner three's time: _____ seconds

# Integrated

# Getting Ready to Speak

**A. Learn the words.**

### Key Vocabulary

| | |
|---|---|
| education | activities related to learning |
| pointless | having no purpose |
| concern | a cause for worry |

### TOEFL Vocabulary

| | |
|---|---|
| announce | to say something publicly |
| available | able to be contacted |
| frequent | to visit regularly |
| appoint | to assign a duty to |
| random | without a plan; no pattern |

**B. Read the announcement. Then answer the questions.**

> **New Study Center**
>
> We are pleased to announce the opening of the Bower Study Center on September 12th. The center will be open from 9 a.m. until 9 p.m. every day of the week. Students will have access to computers. Student tutors will be available to help students with homework. We encourage students to frequent the center regularly.

1. What will happen?
   A new _____.
2. What services will it offer?
   _____ will be available.
3. What do you think the conversation will be about?
   I think the conversation will be about _____.

**Now practice the questions and answers with a partner.**

**C. Listen and repeat.** Track 29

# Practice

## Announcement

**A. Read the announcement again and underline the key information.**

### New Study Center

We are pleased to announce the opening of the Bower Study Center on September 12th. The center will be open from 9 a.m. until 9 p.m. every day of the week. Students will have access to computers. Student tutors will be available to help students with homework. We encourage students to frequent the center regularly.

## Note-taking

**B. Listen to the conversation and take notes.** [Track 30]

| Man | Woman |
|---|---|
| • New study center will be _____ <br> • More access to _____ <br> • Get help with _____ <br> _____ | • Idea is _____ <br> • Not enough _____ <br> • Students will have to _____ <br> • Only get _____ <br> _____ <br> • Helpers appointed _____ <br> • Better to use money for _____ <br> _____ |

## Prompt

**C. Read the prompt.**

The woman expresses her opinion about the announcement made by the university. State her opinion and explain the reasons she gives for holding this opinion.

**D. Listen to the sample response and complete the outline.** Track 31

The conversation is about _____.

A. The man says

    **1.** There will be _____

    **2.** There will be student _____

B. The woman says

    **1.** There are not enough _____

    **2.** Students will _____

    **3.** They will only have _____

C. She says that the university should _____

_____

## Speaking Practice

**E. Now work with a partner. Take turns saying your own response using the outline from above.**

Your time: _____ seconds      Your partner's time: _____ seconds

## TOEFL Vocabulary Practice

**F. Fill in the blanks with the correct words.**

| frequent | randomly | appointed | announced | available |
|---|---|---|---|---|

**1.** Important events are often _____ in the newspapers.

**2.** Most government services are only _____ during business hours.

**3.** Lottery numbers are chosen _____.

**4.** The Secretary of State is _____ by the President, not elected by the people.

**5.** This is one of the cafés that the famous writer used to _____.

# Test

## Step 1

Read the announcement.

**Cancellation of Free Tutoring Services**

We regret to announce that the free tutoring service will no longer be available to students. We have had to stop the service due to lack of funds. We apologize to those students who used the free service. If you are able to pay a tutor for help, that can be arranged at student services.

## Step 2

🎧 Listen to the conversation and take notes. `Track 32`

| Man | Woman |
|---|---|
| • No more _____ <br> • Wouldn't want them to _____ <br> _____ <br> • Students too _____ <br> • Advises woman to write to _____ <br> _____ | • Thinks it's _____ <br> • Better to spend _____ <br> • Education should come _____ <br> • Many students _____ <br> _____ <br> • Professors will have _____ , <br> _____ |

## Step 3

Read the prompt.

The woman expresses her opinion of the announcement made about stopping the free tutoring service. State her opinion and explain the reasons she gives for holding that opinion.

## Step 4

Create an outline for your response.

The conversation is about _____.

    A.  The woman's opinion of this is _____

    B.  She says that the university should _____

        **1.**  give less _____

        **2.**  give more _____

    C.  She thinks this because

        **1.**  education should be _____

        **2.**  a lot of students _____

## Step 5

Write a response using your outline from above.

> The conversation is about _____.
>
> The woman thinks that _____.
>
> Instead, the university should _____ and
>
> _____.
>
> This is because she thinks _____.
>
> She adds that _____.

 **Work with a partner. Take turns saying your response. Then change partners two more times. Time yourselves!**

Your time: _____ seconds      Partner one's time: _____ seconds

Your time: _____ seconds      Partner two's time: _____ seconds

Your time: _____ seconds      Partner three's time: _____ seconds

# Check-up

**Fill in the blanks with the correct words.**

| athletic | energizes | focus | education | pointless | concerned |

1. I volunteer at the homeless shelter because I am _____ about poor people.

2. I am healthy because I lead an _____ lifestyle.

3. I love helping people learn. That's why I want to have a career in _____.

4. A healthy meal always _____ me.

5. Some mothers stay home to _____ on raising their children.

6. A large number of young people feel that voting is _____.

# [ 06 ] Independent

# Getting Ready to Speak

## A. Learn the words.

### Key Vocabulary

| | |
|---|---|
| spend | to pay money |
| concert | a live musical performance |
| save | accumulate money |

### TOEFL Vocabulary

| | |
|---|---|
| spare | extra |
| fashion | clothing style |
| modern | new; trendy |
| allow | let something happen |
| emergency | sudden crisis that needs attention |

## B. Read the prompt. Then answer the questions.

Talk about what you do with your money.

1.  What do you usually buy?
    I usually buy _____.

2.  How do you normally get your money?
    I normally get money from _____.

3.  In the future, what do you want to buy?
    In the future, I want to buy _____.

Now practice the questions and answers with a partner.

C. Listen and repeat. Track 33

# Practice

## Prompt 1

A. **Read the prompt. Then take turns answering the questions with a partner.**

> Talk about the best things to spend money on.

1. What is the best thing you have bought?
2. What are you happy that you spent money on?
3. Is there something that you wish you hadn't spent your money on? Why?
4. What is one thing that you are excited to spend money on in the future? Why?

B. **Make a list of words and phrases related to buying with your classmates.**

_____

_____

_____

_____

## Prompt 2

C. **Read the prompt. Then complete the answers with your own information.**

> Talk about something that you wasted your money on.

| | |
|---|---|
| What? | One time that I wasted money was when _____. |
| When? | I bought this _____. |
| Why? | I bought this thing because _____. |
| Why? | I wasted my money because _____. |

**Now practice your answers with a partner.**

D. **Make a list of words and phrases related to wasting money with a partner.**

_____

_____

_____

_____

**E.  Read the prompt. Then underline the phrases you could use in your own response.**

> Some people spend their spare money, others save their spare money. In your opinion, what is the best thing to do with spare money?

**Reasons for spending or not spending money**

- savings goal
- earn money later
- want it now
- have one time opportunity
- future
- useless

## Sample Response and Outline

**F.  Listen to the sample responses and complete the outlines.**  `Track 34`

### Sample response 1

**First reason:**
_____
_____
_____

**Second reason:**
_____
_____
_____

**What to do with it:**
_____
_____

**This is good because:** _____
_____

### Sample response 2

**First reason:**
_____
_____
_____

**Second reason:**
_____
_____
_____

**What to do with it:**
_____
_____

**This is good because:** _____
_____

## TOEFL Vocabulary Practice

**G. Fill in the blanks with the correct words.**

| fashion | emergency | spare | modern | allow |
|---------|-----------|-------|--------|-------|

1. Parents do not usually _____ children to eat candy before dinner.
2. Many poor countries do not have very _____ technology.
3. The police and fire department are examples of _____ services.
4. It is a good idea to keep a _____ tire in your car.
5. There are many magazines devoted to _____.

# Test

## Step 1

Read the prompt.

> Some people spend their spare money, others save their spare money. In your opinion, what is the best thing to do with spare money?

## Step 2

Create an outline for your response.

⬭ _____

**First reason:**
_____
_____
_____

**Second reason:**
_____
_____
_____

**Benefits:**
_____
_____

**Why this is good:** _____
_____

## Step 3

Write a response using your outline from above.

I think that it is better to _____ your money.
I like to _____ my money.
It is good to have money for _____.
Last year, I _____.
I also like to _____
_____ my money is good because _____.

### Extension

👤👤 **Work with a partner. Take turns saying your response. Then change partners two more times. Time yourselves!**

Your time: _____ seconds       Partner one's time: _____ seconds
Your time: _____ seconds       Partner two's time: _____ seconds
Your time: _____ seconds       Partner three's time: _____ seconds

# Integrated

# Getting Ready to Speak

## A. Learn the words.

### Key Vocabulary

| | |
|---|---|
| astronomer | a person who studies objects in outer space |
| crater | a large hole caused by an explosion or high-speed collision |
| telescope | a device for looking at distant objects |

### TOEFL Vocabulary

| | |
|---|---|
| universe | all matter and energy in space |
| explosion | the act of blowing up, bursting, or exploding |
| sphere | a globe; any object similar in shape to a ball |
| altogether | with everything included |
| consider | to judge; to have an opinion or point of view on something |

## B. Read the passage. Then answer the questions.

### Astronomy

Astronomy is the study of the universe. Astronomers say the universe began with an explosion. They study the planets and stars in our solar system. The Sun is at the center of it. The Sun is a giant sphere of burning gas. We live on a planet called Earth. The Earth has one moon. The moon is covered in craters and it orbits the Earth. All the planets are spheres. There are eight planets in our solar system altogether. There used to be nine, but Pluto is no longer considered to be a planet.

1. What is astronomy the study of?
   Astronomy is the study of the _____.
2. What do astronomers study?
   Astronomers study the _____.
3. What do you think the lecture will be about?
   I think the lecture will be about _____.

👤👤 Now practice the questions and answers with a partner.

🎧 C. Listen and repeat. Track 35

# Practice

**A. Read the passage again and underline the key information.**

> ### Astronomy
> Astronomy is the study of the universe. Astronomers say the universe began with an explosion. They study the planets and stars in our solar system. The Sun is at the center of it. The Sun is a giant sphere of burning gas. We live on a planet called Earth. The Earth has one moon. The moon is covered in craters and it orbits the Earth. All the planets are spheres. There are eight planets in our solar system altogether. There used to be nine, but Pluto is no longer considered to be a planet.

## Note-taking

**B. Listen to the lecture and take notes.** `Track 36`

### Astronomy

- Astronomers look at _____
- They use _____

### Telescopes

- They are used because _____
- Light takes _____
- Sun is bright because _____

### How many planets now?

- There are _____

## Prompt

**C. Read the prompt.**

The professor and the reading passage give details about astronomy and the solar system. Explain what the solar system looks like.

**D. Listen to the sample response and complete the outline.** `Track 37`

The lecture and passage were about astronomy and the solar system.

    A. Astronomers study

        **1.** the _____

        **2.** the size of planets and _____

    B. Planets

        **1.** There used to be nine, now _____

        **2.** We use telescopes because _____

    C. The planets are _____

## Speaking Practice

**E. Now work with a partner. Take turns saying your own response using the outline from above.**

Your time: _____ seconds      Your partner's time: _____ seconds

## TOEFL Vocabulary Practice

**F. Fill in the blanks with the correct words.**

| explosions | altogether | consider | spheres | universe |
|---|---|---|---|---|

**1.** What would you _____ to be your favorite song?

**2.** All of the planets in our solar system are shaped like _____.

**3.** We caught ten fish _____.

**4.** Astronomers study the planets, moons, and stars that make up the

    _____.

**5.** The children were excited by the loud _____ at the fireworks show.

## Step 1

Read the passage.

### The Moon

Many planets have moons. Ours is called Luna. It goes around the Earth once every twenty-seven days. It is covered in big holes called craters. These happen when big rocks in space bang into it. It is the second brightest thing in the sky. The Sun is the brightest. Some people have even walked on the moon.

## Step 2

Listen to the lecture and take notes. Track 38

**The moon**

- orbits _____
- takes _____
- is the _____

**You can**

- see it with _____
- see a full _____
- use a telescope to _____

**When**

- it is bright because we see _____
- it goes between us and the Sun _____
- we always see _____

## Step 3

Read the prompt.

The professor and the reading passage talk about the moon. Explain where the moon moves and what it looks like.

## Step 4

Create an outline for your response.

The passage and lecture were about the moon.

    A. The moon

        **1.** orbits _____

        **2.** takes _____

        **3.** is the only object _____

    B. You can

        **1.** see it _____

        **2.** see a full moon _____

        **3.** use a telescope _____

        **4.** always see the same _____

    C. It is covered in _____

## Step 5

Write a response using your outline from above.

> The passage and lecture were about _____.
> It orbits the _____. It takes _____ to do this.
> You only see a _____ once a month.
> You can see it clearly with your _____.
> When you do see it, you always see _____.
> It is _____.

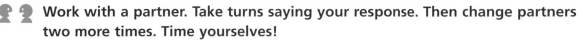

**Work with a partner. Take turns saying your response. Then change partners two more times. Time yourselves!**

Your time: _____ seconds      Partner one's time: _____ seconds

Your time: _____ seconds      Partner two's time: _____ seconds

Your time: _____ seconds      Partner three's time: _____ seconds

# Check-up

**Fill in the blanks with the correct words.**

| save | craters | telescopes | concerts | spend | astronomers |
|------|---------|------------|----------|-------|-------------|

1. Many people _____ money by putting it in the bank.
2. We need to use _____ to look at planets because they are far away.
3. The _____ on the moon were caused by meteorites colliding with it.
4. Many people like to _____ a lot of money while on vacation.
5. People who study the universe are called _____.
6. Many people like to go to _____ to see music performed live.

# [ Review 1 ]

## Step 1

Read the prompt.

> Some people like to study on their own. Others like to study with friends. What do you prefer? Why?

## Step 2

Create an outline for your response.

⟨ _____ ⟩

**Studying on your own**
Benefits:

_____          _____
_____          _____

Drawbacks:

_____          _____
_____          _____

**Studying with friends**

**Better because:** _____
_____

## Step 3

Write a response using your outline from above.

When I study, I prefer to do it _____.
I like it because _____.
It can have disadvantages, though; you _____.
I prefer not to study _____ because
_____.
Studying _____ is better because _____
_____.

👤👤 **Work with a partner. Take turns saying your response. Then change partners two more times. Time yourselves!**

Your time: _____ seconds          Partner one's time: _____ seconds
Your time: _____ seconds          Partner two's time: _____ seconds
Your time: _____ seconds          Partner three's time: _____ seconds

## Step 1

Read the announcement.

> ### Closure of the School Cafeteria
> At the end of the month, the school cafeteria will be closing down. This is due to a lack of interest from students. The area will be off limits after it closes. Students will still be allowed to leave campus at lunch time. Students will also be able to buy snacks and drinks from the school shop.

## Step 2

Listen to the conversation and take notes. **Track 39**

| Man | Woman |
|---|---|
| • The announcement is _____ <br> • For lunch, he goes _____ <br> _____ <br> • At the cafeteria, he _____ <br> _____ <br> • Thinks the school should stop ____ <br> _____ <br> • He wants to _____ <br> _____ | • Did not _____ <br> • Goes to _____ <br> • Suggests that the man could ____ <br> _____ <br> • She thinks that the school _____ <br> _____ |

## Step 3

Read the prompt.

> The man expresses his opinion of the announcement made about the school cafeteria closing. State his opinion and explain the reasons he gives for holding that opinion.

## Step 4

Create an outline for your response.

The conversation is about _____.

    A. The man's opinion of this is that it is a _____

    B. He says that this is because

        **1.** he uses the _____

        **2.** he likes to _____

    C. He says that he should

        **1.** talk to some _____

        **2.** speak to the school and _____

## Step 5

Write a response using your outline from above.

> He thinks closing the school cafeteria is _____.
> This is because _____.
> In addition to eating there, _____.
> He says that _____.
> He also wants to _____ _____
> _____ _____.

### Extension

👤👤 **Work with a partner. Take turns saying your response. Then change partners two more times. Time yourselves!**

Your time: _____ seconds      Partner one's time: _____ seconds

Your time: _____ seconds      Partner two's time: _____ seconds

Your time: _____ seconds      Partner three's time: _____ seconds

## Step 1

Listen to the lecture and take notes. **Track 40**

- A business is a company
- It sells _____
- They can be very _____
- Most start _____
- When Google started, its office _____
- Over time, and when its _____ it became more popular
- Now it is known _____
- A company is better when its _____

## Step 2

Read the prompt.

> The professor describes how businesses can become better. Using points and examples from the lecture, describe the ways that businesses can become more successful.

## Step 3

Create an outline for your response.

The lecture is about businesses and improving them over time.

    A. In the beginning
        **1.** companies are _____
        **2.** do not make much _____

    B. Over time
        **1.** they become _____
        **2.** goods and services _____

    C. Google is a company that
        **1.** began _____
        **2.** is now known and used _____

Conclusion: Businesses take time to improve and get better.

## Step 4

Write a response using your outline.

The lecture is about _____.
In the beginning, businesses _____.
However, over time _____
_____.
Google is an example of a _____
_____.
Businesses take time to _____.

**Work with a partner. Take turns saying your response. Then change partners two more times. Time yourselves!**

Your time: _____ seconds        Partner one's time: _____ seconds
Your time: _____ seconds        Partner two's time: _____ seconds
Your time: _____ seconds        Partner three's time: _____ seconds

## Step 1

Read the prompt.

> Most students have a favorite teacher. Some students like teachers to be fun. Others like teachers to be strict. Describe what your favorite teacher is like.

## Step 2

Create an outline for your response.

_____

**Fun teachers**                    **Strict teachers**
Good points:

_____            _____
_____            _____
_____            _____

Bad points:

_____            _____
_____            _____

**I prefer:** _____

_____

## Step 3

Write a response using your outline from above.

When I am in class, I like to _____.
I like _____ teachers because _____.
I don't like _____ teachers because _____.
My favorite kind of teacher is _____
because _____
_____.

👤👤 **Work with a partner. Take turns saying your response. Then change partners two more times. Time yourselves!**

Your time: _____ seconds          Partner one's time: _____ seconds
Your time: _____ seconds          Partner two's time: _____ seconds
Your time: _____ seconds          Partner three's time: _____ seconds

# [ 07 ] Independent

# Getting Ready to Speak

## A. Learn the words.

### Key Vocabulary

| | |
|---|---|
| correct | accurate; without errors |
| subject | topic of study |
| feelings | something felt emotionally |

### TOEFL Vocabulary

| | |
|---|---|
| achieve | succeed in doing |
| particular | one of several |
| humanities | subjects such as art, language, writing, reading, and music |
| express | to show your thoughts and emotions |
| inspirational | stimulation to do something |

## B. Read the prompt. Then answer the questions.

Talk about your favorite and least favorite subjects in school.

1. What is your favorite subject in school? Why?
   My favorite subject is _____
   because _____.

2. What is your least favorite subject in school?
   My least favorite subject is _____
   because _____.

Now practice the questions and answers with a partner.

C. Listen and repeat. Track 41

# Practice

Prompt 1

A. **Read the prompt. Then take turns answering the questions with a partner.**

> **Talk about your science class.**

1. Do you like your science class?
2. What experiments do you do in class?
3. How well do you normally do in this class?
4. What useful things do you learn in science class?

B. **Make a list of science related words and phrases with your classmates.**

_____

_____

_____

_____

Prompt 2

C. **Read the prompt. Then complete the answers with your own information.**

> **Talk about your art and music classes.**

Which class?   I prefer going to _____.

What?          My favorite kind of art to make is _____.

How often?     I practice music _____.

What?          I play _____.

**Now practice your answers with a partner.**

D. **Make a list of music and art related words and phrases with a partner.**

_____

_____

_____

_____

**E.  Read the prompt. Then underline the phrases you could use in your own response.**

> Some people are good at math and science. Others are better at art and music. What are you good at? Do you like that subject? Why?

**Reasons to like a class**

- no wrong answers
- easier to find a job
- much more useful
- helps to understand people
- allows more creativity
- much more organized

## Sample Response and Outline

**F.  Listen to the sample responses and complete the outlines.**  Track 42

| Sample response 1 | Sample response 2 |
|---|---|

_(circle)_

**First reason:** _____ **Second reason:** _____  **First reason:** _____ **Second reason:** _____

_____ _____  _____ _____
_____ _____  _____ _____
_____ _____  _____ _____

**Like because:** _____  **Like because:** _____

_____ _____  _____ _____
_____ _____  _____ _____

**I prefer:** _____  **I prefer:** _____

_____  _____

## TOEFL Vocabulary Practice

**G.  Fill in the blanks with the correct words.**

| achieve | particular | humanities | express | inspirational |
|---|---|---|---|---|

**1.** John F. Kennedy was a very _____ speaker.

**2.** People often _____ success after many years of failure.

**3.** Chemistry and biology are not _____ subjects.

**4.** People can often remember _____ days in their past that were important to them.

**5.** A successful actor can _____ many different emotions.

# Test

## Step 1

Read the prompt.

> Some people are good at math and science. Others are better at art and music.
> What are you good at? Do you like that subject? Why?

## Step 2

Create an outline for your response.

_____

**First reason:**

_____

_____

_____

**Second reason:**

_____

_____

_____

**Like because:** _____

_____

**I prefer:** _____

_____

## Step 3

Write a response using your outline from above.

I like _____.
I think these subjects _____.
I think they help me _____.
I especially like _____.
I like to _____, so this class is good for me.
I usually _____ to study hard for these subjects because _____
_____.

**Extension**

 **Work with a partner. Take turns saying your response. Then change partners
two more times. Time yourselves!**

Your time: _____ seconds        Partner one's time: _____ seconds
Your time: _____ seconds        Partner two's time: _____ seconds
Your time: _____ seconds        Partner three's time: _____ seconds

# Integrated

## Getting Ready to Speak

**A. Learn the words.**

| | |
|---|---|
| vacation | holiday or time off from work or school |
| definitely | certainly; for sure |
| decision | choice |

**TOEFL Vocabulary**

| | |
|---|---|
| responsibility | requiring reliability or dependability |
| culture | the shared beliefs and values of a group |
| relax | spend time at ease |
| interests | things one likes doing |
| youth | time of one's life when one is young |

**B. Listen to the first part of a conversation. Then answer the questions.** `Track 43`

1. What are the students discussing?
   The students are discussing _____.

2. What would be the advantages of going abroad?
   The student says _____.

3. What do you think the rest of the conversation will be about?
   I think the rest of the conversation will be about _____
   _____.

4. What do you think the student should do?
   I think the student should _____
   _____.

**Now practice the questions and answers with a partner.**

**C. Listen and repeat.** `Track 44`

# Practice

**Note-taking**

**A. Listen to the full conversation and take notes.** [Track 45]

| Man | Woman |
|-----|-------|
| • Two choices: _____ _____ | • Working with _____ |
| | • Thinks traveling might be _____ |
| • Traveling might _____ _____ | • He could experience _____ _____ |
| • Doesn't _____ | • Thinks the man could learn _____ |
| • Doesn't have _____ | _____ |
| • Would miss _____ | • Might be nice to _____ |
| • Staying might be _____ | • Could spend time _____ |
| • Won't meet _____ | • Thinks man's summer will be _____ |
| • Could _____ | _____ |

**B. Use your notes to complete the answers.**

**1.** What are some reasons the students discuss for traveling abroad?

The students discuss _____.

**2.** What are some reasons the students discuss about staying home?

The students discuss _____.

**Now practice the questions and answers with a partner.**

**Prompt**

**C. Read the prompt.**

> The students discuss two different possibilities. Describe the advantages of each
> choice. Then state which of the two choices you prefer and why.

**D. Listen to the sample response and complete the outline.** Track 46

The conversation is about _____.

    A. Advantages of traveling abroad
        **1.** Experience _____
        **2.** Visit _____
    B. Disadvantages of traveling abroad
        **1.** Miss _____
        **2.** Can't speak _____
    C. Advantages of staying home
        **1.** _____
        **2.** _____
    D. Disadvantages of staying home
        **1.** _____
        **2.** Wouldn't meet _____
Conclusion: I think _____.

**E. Write your own conclusion using the outline from above.**

Conclusion: I think he should _____

because _____.

## Speaking Practice

**F. Now work with a partner. Take turns saying your own response using the outline from above.**

Your time: _____ seconds      Partner's time: _____ seconds

## TOEFL Vocabulary Practice

**G. Fill in the blanks with the correct words.**

| relax | culture | interests | responsibility | youth |
|-------|---------|-----------|----------------|-------|

**1.** In my _____ I often made bad decisions.

**2.** Having a baby is a big _____.

**3.** Playing soccer is one of my _____.

**4.** I find Asian _____ fascinating.

**5.** After a long week of work, I like to stay home and _____ on weekends.

# Test

## Step 1

**Listen to the conversation and take notes.** Track 47

| Man | Woman |
|---|---|
| • Found a job?<br>• I will work at a _____<br>• I like having _____<br>• I'm saving for _____<br>• I'm going to buy a _____<br>• I have met _____<br>• We have same _____<br>• Hurry if you want to find a good job | • No, I'm not sure<br>• I like having _____<br>• I can _____<br>• Not _____<br>• Having a job is a lot of _____<br>• I want to _____<br>• I want to enjoy my _____ |

## Step 2

Read the prompt.

> The students are discussing summer jobs. Describe the advantages and disadvantages of getting a summer job. Then state if you would like to get one and why.

## Step 3

Create an outline for your response.

The conversation is about _____.

    A. Advantages of having a summer job

        **1.** Can earn _____

             • can buy _____

        **2.** Can make new _____

             • have same _____

    B. Disadvantages of having a summer job

        **1.** No _____

             • have to think about _____

        **2.** A lot of _____

    C. Can't decide

        **1.** Want to _____

        **2.** Also want to _____

Conclusion: I would prefer _____.

## Step 4

Write a response using your outline.

The conversation is about _____.
The male student already has a job at a summer camp. He likes having a summer
job because he can _____
and then he can _____.
Also, he can meet _____ who have _____. The
female student likes her _____ she doesn't have to
_____. Also, having a job is a lot of _____.
She wants to _____ but she also wants to _____.
I would prefer _____.

Extension

**Work with a partner. Take turns saying your answer. Then change partners
two more times. Time yourselves.**

Your time: _____ seconds        Partner one's time: _____ seconds
Your time: _____ seconds        Partner two's time: _____ seconds
Your time: _____ seconds        Partner three's time: _____ seconds

# Check-up

**Fill in the blanks with the correct words.**

| correct | subjects | feelings | decision | definitely | vacation |
|---|---|---|---|---|---|

1. University students have the opportunity to study many different _____.
2. Many people like to travel during their _____.
3. When you are upset, it can help to talk about your _____.
4. The more you study for a test, the more _____ answers you will have.
5. Choosing a university can be a difficult _____.
6. Some people believe that if you exercise and eat right, you will _____ live longer.

# [ 08 ] Independent

## Getting Ready to Speak

**A. Learn the words.**

### Key Vocabulary

| | |
|---|---|
| violent | using physical force; intense |
| behavior | how someone acts or behaves |
| habit | something done all the time |

### TOEFL Vocabulary

| | |
|---|---|
| content | subject matter |
| in addition | also |
| positive | good |
| message | a lesson or important idea that someone wants to communicate |
| reduce | to decrease |

**B. Read the prompt. Then answer the questions.**

| Talk about your TV habits. |
|---|

**1.** What kind of TV shows do you like?
   I like to watch _____.

**2.** How much time each day do you usually watch TV?
   I usually watch TV for _____.

**3.** When do you watch TV?
   I watch TV _____.

👤👤 **Now practice the questions and answers with a partner.**

🎧 **C. Listen and repeat.** `Track 48`

# Practice

Prompt 1

**A. Read the prompt. Then take turns answering the questions with a partner.**

Talk about your favorite TV show.

1. What is your favorite TV show?
2. Who is your favorite person on the show?
3. Why do you like the show so much?
4. Is the show popular with other people? Why?

**B. Make a list of positive television words and phrases with your classmates.**

_____

_____

_____

_____

Prompt 2

**C. Read the prompt. Then complete the answers with your own information.**

What TV show has had a positive or negative influence on you?

| | |
|---|---|
| What? | The TV show that affected me was _____. |
| Where? | I always watch this TV show _____. |
| How? | After watching the show, I _____. |
| Why? | The TV show has changed me because _____. |

**Now practice your answers with a partner.**

**D. Make a list of negative television words and phrases with a partner.**

_____

_____

_____

_____

**E. Read the prompt. Then underline the phrases you could use in your own response.**

> Some people think that TV has a good influence on children. Others think that it has a bad influence on children. What do you think? Why?

**Reasons to think TV has a good or bad influence on children**

- educational
- do not study hard
- fun and exciting
- see new things
- can cause laziness
- no longer exercise

## Sample Response and Outline

**F. Listen to the sample responses and complete the outlines.** `Track 49`

### Sample response 1

_____

**First reason:**
_____
_____
_____

**Second reason:**
_____
_____
_____

**Think this because:**
_____
_____

**Think that:**
_____ _____
_____

### Sample response 2

_____

**First reason:**
_____
_____
_____

**Second reason:**
_____
_____
_____

**Think this because:**
_____
_____

**Think that:** _____
_____

## TOEFL Vocabulary Practice

**G. Fill in the blanks with the correct words.**

| in addition | content | messages | positive | reduce |
|---|---|---|---|---|

1. Many people feel that teachers should have a _____ influence on students.
2. _____ to bananas, apples, and oranges are also fruits.
3. Students sometimes get put into classes where the _____ is much too difficult.
4. Eating healthy is a great way to _____ your chance of becoming sick.
5. Many parents are worried that children are getting the wrong _____ from video games.

# Test

## Step 1

Read the prompt.

> Some people think that TV has a good influence on children. Others think that it has a bad influence on children. What do you think? Why?

## Step 2

Create an outline for your response.

_____

**First reason:**

_____

_____

_____

**Second reason:**

_____

_____

_____

**Think this because:** _____

_____

**Think that:** _____

_____

## Step 3

Write a response using your outline from above.

I think television has a _____ influence on children.
One reason I think this is because _____.
Television can _____.
Children who watch a lot of television _____.
Watching a lot of TV can _____.
TV is _____ because _____.

| Extension |

 **Work with a partner. Take turns saying your response. Then change partners two more times. Time yourselves!**

Your time: _____ seconds     Partner one's time: _____ seconds
Your time: _____ seconds     Partner two's time: _____ seconds
Your time: _____ seconds     Partner three's time: _____ seconds

# Integrated

## Getting Ready to Speak

**A. Learn the words.**

### Key Vocabulary

| | |
|---|---|
| acid | a corrosive substance that can burn |
| float | the upward movement of a light substance |
| mix | combine ingredients; put together |

### TOEFL Vocabulary

| | |
|---|---|
| contain | to hold something inside something else |
| form | to start to exist; to come into being |
| release | to let something go; to free it |
| damage | to hurt, harm, or break |
| structure | the way something is put together |

**B. Listen to the first part of a lecture. Then answer the questions.** Track 50

1. What is the lecture mainly about?
   The lecture is about _____.

2. How is acid rain formed?
   Acid rain is formed when _____.

3. What else do you think the professor will talk about?
   I think the professor will talk about _____.

**Now practice the questions and answers with a partner.**

**C. Listen and repeat.** Track 51

# Practice

A. **Listen to the full lecture and take notes.** `Track 52`

- Acid rain contains sulfur and _____
- It forms when coal, oil, or _____
- We burn coal to make _____
- We use electricity in _____
- We burn oil to make cars go and to _____
- This releases sulfur and nitrogen _____
- The gases mix with _____
- It is bad for plants and _____
- It makes acid rain that is _____
- It is a big _____

B. **Use your notes to complete the answers.**

1. Give one example mentioned by the professor of why we burn coal, oil, and wood.

   The professor gives the example of _____.

2. How does the professor explain the formation of acid rain?

   The professor explains that gases float _____
   and mix with _____ to form _____.

**Now practice the questions and answers with a partner.**

Prompt

C. **Read the prompt.**

> The professor discusses acid rain. Using points and examples from the lecture, describe how acid rain forms and what its effects are.

**D. Listen to the sample response and complete the outline.** `Track 53`

The lecture is about _____.

A. Acid rain forms when we burn

   **1.** _____

   **2.** _____

   **3.** _____

B. We burn these things to

   **1.** make electricity for _____

   **2.** make _____

   **3.** make _____

C. This releases

   **1.** _____

   **2.** _____ gases.

D. The gases float _____ and mix with _____.

Conclusion: Acid rain kills _____ and is

_____.

## Speaking Practice

**E. Now work with a partner. Take turns saying your own response using the outline from above.**

Your time: _____ seconds     Your partner's time: _____ seconds

## TOEFL Vocabulary Practice

**F. Fill in the blanks with the correct words.**

| forms | structure | contains | released | damage |
|---|---|---|---|---|

**1.** If you drink too much alcohol, you can _____ your liver.

**2.** Ice _____ when water is exposed to very cold temperatures.

**3.** Nelson Mandela was _____ from prison in 1990.

**4.** Coca Cola _____ a lot of sugar.

**5.** The _____ of English grammar is difficult to understand.

# Test

## Step 1

Listen to the lecture and take notes. **Track 54**

- Acid rain does a lot of _____
- It damages buildings made of sandstone and _____
- It makes holes in them and damages their _____
- Acid rain hurts plants and animals that _____
- Acid burns them and kills the _____
- It kills fish and fish _____
- Birds _____
- Acid rain damages leaves and _____
- Then plants can't grow because the soil is _____

## Step 2

Read the prompt.

The professor describes how acid rain damages nature and the environment. Using points and examples from the lecture, describe how acid rain does this.

## Step 3

Create an outline for your response.

The lecture is about how acid rain does a lot of harm.

    A. Damage to buildings made of _____
        **1.** by making _____
        **2.** by damaging their _____
    B. Burns or kills water plants and animals
        **1.** Kills insects _____
        **2.** Kills _____
        **3.** Makes _____
    C. Damages forests
        **1.** Damages _____
        **2.** Makes soil too acidic for _____
Conclusion: Acid rain must be stopped.

## Step 4

Write a response using your outline.

Acid rain does _____. It can damage _____
_____.
It burns or kills water _____.
Acid rain kills insects _____.
It kills fish and _____.
It damages forests _____
_____.
Acid rain _____.

Extension

**Work with a partner. Take turns saying your response. Then change partners two more times. Time yourselves!**

Your time: _____ seconds          Partner one's time: _____ seconds

Your time: _____ seconds          Partner two's time: _____ seconds

Your time: _____ seconds          Partner three's time: _____ seconds

# Check-up

**Fill in the blanks with the correct words.**

| violent | behavior | habit | mix | acid | float |

1. You should wear gloves and eye protection if you must handle _____.
2. If you tease a dog, it may respond with a _____ reaction.
3. Smoking is a bad _____.
4. Students should be on their best _____ in school.
5. On a windy day, a feather may _____ up into the air.
6. It is dangerous to _____ fire and gasoline.

# [ 09 ] Independent

# Getting Ready to Speak

## A. Learn the words.

### Key Vocabulary

| | |
|---|---|
| rather | in a more willing way |
| comprehend | to understand |
| success | achievement of a goal; something that turns out well |

### TOEFL Vocabulary

| | |
|---|---|
| manage | to achieve something with some difficulty; to deal with a difficult situation |
| routine | regular; habitual |
| discipline | training that teaches you to obey rules and control your behavior |
| vital | very important |
| challenge | test of ability |

## B. Read the prompt. Then answer the questions.

Talk about your study habits.

1. What kind of environment do you need to study effectively?
   I need _____.

2. Is there anything you like to do while studying? If yes, what?
   I like to _____ while studying.

3. When do you prefer to study?
   I prefer to study _____.

Now practice the questions and answers with a partner.

C. Listen and repeat. Track 55

# Practice

Prompt 1

**A. Read the prompt. Take turns answering the questions with a partner.**

### What do you normally do after school?

1. What time do you finish school every day?
2. What is the first thing you do when you come home?
3. Do you go somewhere else after your school is done? If yes, where?
4. Do you exercise? If yes, what do you do?

**B. Make a list of activity words and phrases with your classmates.**

_____

_____

_____

_____

Prompt 2

**C. Read the prompt. Then complete the answers with your own information.**

### Talk about your daily homework.

| | |
|---|---|
| What subjects? | I usually have homework for _____. |
| Where? | I usually do my homework in/at _____. |
| How much? | I typically have _____ hours of homework every day. |
| Which? | My _____ teacher gives me the most homework. |

**Now practice your answers with a partner.**

**D. Make a list of school work related words and phrases with a partner.**

_____

_____

_____

_____

**E. Read the prompt. Then underline the phrases you could use in your own response.**

> Some people hate doing homework because they find it boring. Others like doing homework because it helps them learn and understand. Do you like doing homework? Why?

**Reasons to like or dislike homework**

- teacher should teach in class
- makes us think
- challenge
- can be very difficult
- causes stress
- reminders

## Sample Response and Outline

**F. Now listen to the sample responses and complete the outlines.** `Track 56`

### Sample response 1

_____

**First reason:** _____ _____ _____

**Second reason:** _____ _____ _____

**Don't like because:** _____ _____ _____

**Think that:** _____ _____

### Sample response 2

_____

**First reason:** _____ _____ _____

**Second reason:** _____ _____ _____

**Like because:** _____ _____ _____

**Think that:** _____ _____

## TOEFL Vocabulary Practice

**G. Fill in the blanks with the correct words.**

| challenge | manage | routine | discipline | vital |
|---|---|---|---|---|

1. Blind people have learned to _____ without being able to see.
2. The army teaches many young people _____.
3. While scuba diving it is _____ to remain calm.
4. Many students look forward to the _____ of university.
5. Most children change their daily _____ during summer vacation.

# Test

## Step 1

Read the prompt.

> Some people hate doing homework because they find it boring. Others like doing homework because it helps them learn and understand. Do you like doing homework? Why?

## Step 2

Create an outline for your response.

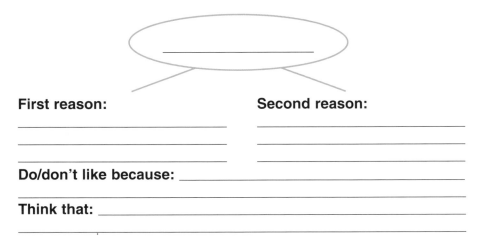

**First reason:**

_____

_____

_____

**Do/don't like because:** _____

_____

**Think that:** _____

_____

**Second reason:**

_____

_____

_____

## Step 3

Write a response using your outline from above.

I _____ homework.

I think homework is _____.

Homework makes me _____.

I would rather _____.

In addition, homework _____.

Homework is _____ because _____.

### Extension

**Work with a partner. Take turns saying your response. Then change partners two more times. Time yourselves!**

Your time: _____ seconds

Your time: _____ seconds

Your time: _____ seconds

Partner one's time: _____ seconds

Partner two's time: _____ seconds

Partner three's time: _____ seconds

# Integrated

## Getting Ready to Speak

### A. Learn the words.

**Key Vocabulary**

| | |
|---|---|
| unexpected | not easily foreseen or predicted |
| timetable | a schedule of classes |
| inform | to tell someone about something |

**TOEFL Vocabulary**

| | |
|---|---|
| demand | a measure of how much people want something |
| conflict | to differ |
| respond | to reply or react to |
| advance | to move ahead |
| dedicated | devoted to a particular purpose |

### B. Read the announcement. Then answer the questions.

> **Change In Office Hours in Health Sciences Department**
>
> The Health Sciences Department has received several complaints regarding the professors' office hours. It seems that our current hours conflict with many students' timetables. We have chosen to respond to these complaints by increasing our office hours. We hope that every student will be able to get the attention he or she needs. Please ask your professors to inform you of their new hours.

1. What will happen?
   The Health Sciences Department will _____.
2. What should students do?
   Students should _____.
3. What do you think the conversation will be about?
   I think the conversation will be about _____.

**Now practice the questions and answers with a partner.**

**C. Listen and repeat.** `Track 57`

# Practice

**A. Read the announcement again and underline the key information.**

> ### Change in Office Hours in Health Sciences Department
> The Health Sciences Department has received several complaints regarding the professors' office hours. It seems that our current hours conflict with many students' timetables. We have chosen to respond to these complaints by increasing our office hours. We hope that every student will be able to get the attention he or she needs. Please ask your professors to inform you of their new hours.

## Note-taking

**B. Listen to the conversation and take notes.** Track 58

| Man | Woman |
|---|---|
| • Professors are _____ <br> • It is only for the _____ <br> _____ <br> • Thinks announcement is _____ <br> • Professor's hours conflict _____ <br> _____ <br> • Always has classes _____ <br> • Lots of students are having _____ <br> • Has to _____ <br> _____ <br> • Needs _____ | • Wants to know if change will affect <br> _____ <br> • Change doesn't help her because she is a _____ |

## Prompt

**C. Read the prompt.**

> The man expresses his opinion about the announcement made by the Health Sciences Department. State his opinion and explain the reasons he gives for holding that opinion.

**D. Listen to the sample response and complete the outline.** `Track 59`

The conversation is about _____.

    A.  The man thinks _____

    B.  He thinks this because

        **1.** he can't see his professors during _____

            _____

        **2.** many other students have _____

            _____

    C.  He needs to get help with _____

Conclusion: He is very _____.

## Speaking Practice

**E. Now work with a partner. Take turns saying your own response using the outline from above.**

Your time: _____ seconds    Your partner's time: _____ seconds

## TOEFL Vocabulary Practice

**F. Fill in the blanks with the correct words.**

| respond | conflicts | advance | dedicated | demand |
|---------|-----------|---------|-----------|--------|

**1.** Because of their popularity, the _____ for cell phones is very high these days.

**2.** He didn't _____ to her cries for help because she had lied so many times before.

**3.** My new program won't run because it _____ with my computer.

**4.** '911' is a _____ emergency services telephone number.

**5.** The soccer team had to win the next game if they wished to _____ to the final.

# Test

## Step 1

Read the announcement.

### New Study Group Rooms in Library

The Fitzgerald Library is pleased to announce that starting in September, fifteen of our rooms will be dedicated to study groups. These are small rooms with a large, round table which is excellent for group study. Study groups can reserve a room at the front desk by filling out a form. Be sure to do so in advance as demand for these rooms will be high.

## Step 2

Listen to the conversation and take notes. Track 60

| Man | Woman |
| --- | --- |
| • Wants to form a _____ _____ | • Thinks it's a good idea, so wants to discuss _____ |
| • Wonders where they can _____ | • Suggests the _____ because _____ |
| • Thinks the news is _____ | • Can't go to _____ |
| • His literature group meets in the ___ _____ | • Might _____ |
| • Problem there is it gets _____ | |
| • Suggests they _____ _____ | |

## Step 3

Read the prompt.

The man expresses his opinion of the announcement made about the library having dedicated study group rooms. State his opinion and explain the reasons he gives for holding that opinion.

## Step 4

Create an outline for your response.

The conversation is about _____.

    A.  The man's opinion of this is _____

    B.  He thinks this because his study group _____

        _____

    C.  You can't have discussions _____

        _____

## Step 5

Write a response using your outline from above.

> He thinks dedicating rooms in the library to study groups is _____
> _____.
> Right now his study group _____.
> But he doesn't like it because _____.
> That's why he _____. The woman adds that you
> can't _____.
> This is because you might _____.

**Work with a partner. Take turns saying your response. Then change partners two more times. Time yourselves!**

Your time: _____ seconds      Partner one's time: _____ seconds

Your time: _____ seconds      Partner two's time: _____ seconds

Your time: _____ seconds      Partner three's time: _____ seconds

# Check-up

**Fill in the blanks with the correct words.**

| rather | comprehend | success | unexpected | timetable | inform |
|--------|-----------|---------|-----------|-----------|--------|

1. I just received my _____. It's great! I don't have any classes before noon!

2. Many people would _____ pay someone to paint their home than to do it themselves.

3. People who study art in college often find it difficult to _____ high level science.

4. The Apollo moon landings were a great _____.

5. She wasn't prepared for his _____ visit, but she was happy to see him.

6. If you plan to visit someone, it is polite to _____ them first.

# [ 10 ] Independent

## Getting Ready to Speak

### A. Learn the words.

**Key Vocabulary**

| | |
|---|---|
| lifestyle | how a person lives |
| increase | to go up |
| waste | to not use something wisely or properly |

**TOEFL Vocabulary**

| | |
|---|---|
| necessity | something needed; something essential |
| maintain | to make something continue |
| balance | to have an equal amount on either side |
| suggest | to recommend or remind someone of something |
| optional | not required to do; not obligatory |

### B. Read the prompt. Then answer the questions.

**Talk about what you like to do in gym class.**

1. Do you like gym class? Why?
   I _____ gym class because _____.

2. What is your favorite part of gym class?
   My favorite part of gym class is _____.

3. What is your least favorite part of gym class?
   My least favorite part of gym class is _____.

**Now practice the questions and answers with a partner.**

C. **Listen and repeat.** Track 61

# Practice

**Prompt 1**

**A. Read the prompt. Then take turns answering the questions with a partner.**

> Is exercise important to you? Why?

1. What do you like to do for exercise?
2. How often do you exercise?
3. How do you feel after you exercise?
4. Does exercise help you? Why?

**B. Make a list of exercise words and phrases with your classmates.**

_____

_____

_____

_____

**Prompt 2**

**C. Read the prompt. Then complete the answers with your own information.**

> When should children exercise?

| | |
|---|---|
| Where? | Children should exercise _____. |
| How often? | Children should exercise _____. |
| What? | Children should _____ when they exercise. |
| Why? | They should exercise because _____. |

**Now practice your answers with a partner.**

**D. Make a list of sports words and phrases with a partner.**

_____

_____

_____

_____

**E. Read the prompt. Then underline the phrases you could use in your own response.**

> Many people think that physical education should be required in schools and colleges. What do you think? Why?

**Reasons for and against physical education in school**

- waste of time
- makes kids healthy
- helps kids focus
- costs the school money
- not useful for future jobs
- teaches important habits

## Sample Response and Outline

**F. Listen to the sample responses and complete the outlines.** `Track 62`

**Sample response 1**

⬭ _____

**First reason:** _____  _____ _____

**Second reason:** _____ _____ _____

**Should do this:** _____ _____ _____ _____

**Think that:** _____ _____

**Sample response 2**

⬭ _____

**First reason:** _____ _____ _____

**Second reason:** _____ _____ _____

**Should do this:** _____ _____ _____ _____

**Think that:** _____ _____

## TOEFL Vocabulary Practice

**G. Fill in the blanks with the correct words.**

| maintained | balance | necessity | suggest | optional |
|---|---|---|---|---|

1. Roman soldiers always _____ their bravery, even when faced with danger.

2. Specialized training is a _____ for firefighters.

3. Gymnasts can often _____ on their hands for a very long time.

4. Even if you don't have to, completing _____ homework will better prepare you for tests.

5. A good salesperson will _____ which kind of clothes will look best on a person.

# Test

## Step 1

Read the prompt.

> Many people think that physical education should be required in schools and colleges. What do you think? Why?

## Step 2

Create an outline for your response.

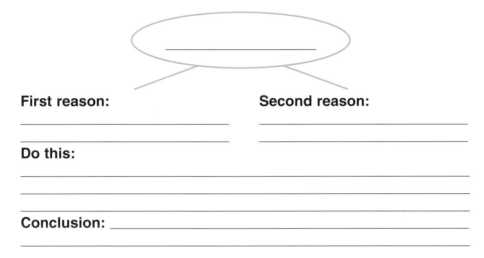

**First reason:** _____  **Second reason:** _____

_____  _____

**Do this:**

_____

_____

_____

**Conclusion:** _____

_____

## Step 3

Write a response using your outline from above.

I think that _____.

Physical education is _____.

Exercise is important because _____

_____.

P.E. doesn't _____.

P.E. is/isn't necessary because _____.

### Extension

👥 **Work with a partner. Take turns saying your response. Then change partners two more times. Time yourselves!**

Your time: _____ seconds    Partner one's time: _____ seconds

Your time: _____ seconds    Partner two's time: _____ seconds

Your time: _____ seconds    Partner three's time: _____ seconds

# Integrated

## Getting Ready to Speak

### A. Learn the words.

**Key Vocabulary**

| | |
|---|---|
| huge | very big in size |
| theater | place where movies or plays are shown |
| remote control | handheld device used to operate electronic devices from a distance |

**TOEFL Vocabulary**

| | |
|---|---|
| channel | TV or radio station |
| currently | now; at present |
| gradual | developing slowly |
| progress | the development or improvement of something |
| entertainment | the different ways of keeping people amused and entertained |

### B. Read the passage. Then answer the questions.

> **Technology**
>
> Currently, technology is a huge part of entertainment. People all over the world can watch television or listen to the radio. It was first used in the entertainment business almost 100 years ago. Before television and radio, people would read, tell stories, play music, or go to the theater for fun. Because of the progress of technology, we can now do all of these things at home.

1. What technologies can people use all over the world nowadays?
   People can watch _____ and listen to _____.
2. What did people used to do for fun before television and radio were used for entertainment?
   People used to _____.
3. What do you think the lecture will be about?
   I think the lecture will be about _____.

**Now practice the questions and answers with a partner.**

**C. Listen and repeat.** Track 63

# Practice

**A. Read the passage again and underline the key information.**

> ### Technology
>
> Currently, technology is a huge part of entertainment. People all over the world can watch television or listen to the radio. It was first used in the entertainment business almost 100 years ago. Before television and radio, people would read, tell stories, play music, or go to the theater for fun. Because of the progress of technology, we can now do all of these things at home.

## Note-taking

**B. Listen to the lecture and take notes.** `Track 64`

**Technology**

- The effect on our lives _____
- Before it, people were _____
- Now we have _____

**Examples**

- We can use the _____
- We use them for _____
- Outside we can _____
- We can even watch _____

**Technology**

- Progress _____
- It is easy to have fun _____
- We do not have to _____

## Prompt

**C. Read the prompt.**

> The professor and the passage give details about technology in entertainment. Describe how the things that people do for fun have changed because of technology.

**D. Listen to the sample response and complete the outline.** `Track 65`

The lecture and passage were about _____.

    A. It has a huge effect on _____

    B. In the past

        **1.** people used to _____

        **2.** they did this _____

    C. Nowadays

        **1.** we also _____

        **2.** we can even do this _____

    D. Things are changing _____

    E. Because of technology, we can do _____

## Speaking Practice

**E. Now work with a partner. Take turns saying your own response using the outline from above.**

Your time: _____ seconds          Partner's time: _____ seconds

## TOEFL Vocabulary Practice

**F. Fill in the blanks with the correct words.**

| currently | entertainment | channel | gradually | progress |
|---|---|---|---|---|

**1.** Many people think the best form of _____ is TV.

**2.** Unfortunately, the hole in my shirt is _____ getting worse.

**3.** I am making good _____ with my report.

**4.** CNN is a popular TV news _____.

**5.** _____, there is no cure for cancer.

# Test

## Step 1

Read the passage.

### Television

Television is an electronic device that shows us moving pictures and plays sounds at the same time. It became popular in the late 1930s. It is still hugely popular today. Many people use it for entertainment and news. Many homes have one or more TVs in them. With cable and satellite TV, you can choose whatever you want to watch on your TV.

## Step 2

Listen to the lecture and take notes. `Track 66`

**Television**

- lets us see _____
- lets us hear _____

**To begin with**

- there were only _____
- they were _____
- pictures were in _____

**As technology moves on**

- we can watch and record _____
- you can choose what each one _____
- people can buy _____
- you can play _____

**In the future**

- you will be able to _____

## Step 3

Read the prompt.

The professor and the passage talk about television and entertainment. Explain why the television is an important part of entertainment technology.

## Step 4

Create an outline for your response.

The passage and lecture were about television and entertainment.

- A.  Television became popular _____
    - 1.  The pictures were _____
    - 2.  It lets us see _____
- B.  With TV today
    - 1.  You can watch _____
    - 2.  You can play _____
- C.  In the future
    - 1.  You will be able to do _____
    - 2.  You will have _____

## Step 5

Write a response using your outline from above.

> The passage and lecture were about _____.
> Television became popular _____.
> To begin with, the pictures were _____.
> Television lets us see _____ and hear _____.
> With TV today you can watch and record _____.
> On a TV, you can play _____.
> In the future you will be able to do _____.
> You will have even _____.

### Extension

**Work with a partner. Take turns saying your response. Then change partners two more times. Time yourselves!**

Your time: _____ seconds        Partner one's time: _____ seconds

Your time: _____ seconds        Partner two's time: _____ seconds

Your time: _____ seconds        Partner three's time: _____ seconds

# Check-up

**Fill in the blanks with the correct words.**

> waste　　lifestyle　　increase　　remote control　　huge　　theater

1. I cannot find the _____. Have you seen it?
2. If you win the lottery, you should be able to improve your _____.
3. Buying something and then not using it is a _____ of money.
4. A blue whale is a _____ mammal that lives in the sea.
5. Scientists are worried about the _____ in the Earth's average temperature.
6. If you work in a _____, you can watch movies for free.

# [ 11 ] Independent

## Getting Ready to Speak

### A. Learn the words.

**Key Vocabulary**

| | |
|---|---|
| despise | to hate something |
| hectic | constantly busy and hurried |
| late | not on time |

**TOEFL Vocabulary**

| | |
|---|---|
| supposed to | required to do something |
| located | in a specific place |
| mode | method; style |
| require | to need |
| effort | activity done to accomplish a goal |

### B. Read the prompt. Then answer the questions.

Talk about traveling by land (car, train, bus, etc) or by sea.

**1.** What do you dislike about traveling by land?
I dislike _____.

**2.** What is an advantage about traveling by sea?
An advantage of traveling by sea is _____.

**3.** What is an advantage of traveling by land?
An advantage of traveling by land is _____.

👤👤 **Now practice the questions and answers with a partner.**

🎧 C. **Listen and repeat.** Track 67

# Practice

## Prompt 1

 **A. Read the prompt. Then take turns answering the questions with a partner.**

Talk about traveling on an airplane.

1. Have you been on an airplane?
2. What do you do (or would you do) during the flight?
3. How do you feel (or would you feel) after flying?
4. Do you like (or would you like) flying in an airplane? Why?

**B. Make a list of traveling words and phrases with your classmates.**

_____

_____

_____

_____

## Prompt 2

**C. Read the prompt. Then complete the answers with your own information.**

Talk about your last vacation.

| | |
|---|---|
| What did you do? | I _____. |
| Where did you go? | I went to _____. |
| How did you get there? | I got there by _____. |
| Who? | I went with _____. |

**Now practice your answers with a partner.**

**D. Make a list of vacation related words and phrases with a partner.**

_____

_____

_____

_____

**E. Read the prompt. Then underline the phrases you could use in your own response.**

When going on a vacation, some people like to travel by airplane because it is fast. Others like to travel by train or boat because they get to see more. What mode of transport do you prefer? Why?

**Reasons to prefer one type of transport over another**

- convenient
- relaxing
- not scared
- no motion sickness
- centrally located
- more leg room
- less crowded
- fast and easy

## Sample Response and Outline

**F. Listen to the sample responses and complete the outlines.** `Track 68`

### Sample response 1

_____

**First reason:**
_____
_____
_____

**Second reason:**
_____
_____
_____

**Like because:**
_____
_____

**Think that:** _____
_____

### Sample response 2

_____

**First reason:**
_____
_____
_____

**Second reason:**
_____
_____
_____

**Like because:**
_____
_____

**Think that:** _____
_____

## TOEFL Vocabulary Practice

**G. Fill in the blanks with the correct words.**

| mode | supposed to | located | require | effort |
|------|-------------|---------|---------|--------|

1. It takes skill and _____ to be a successful professional athlete.
2. London is _____ in England.
3. The subway is a fast and convenient _____ of transportation.
4. You are _____ turn off your cell phone in the movie theater.
5. US high schools _____ all their students to pass an exam before leaving.

# Test

## Step 1

Read the prompt.

> When going on a vacation, some people like to travel by airplane because it is fast. Others like to travel by train or boat because they get to see more. What mode of transport do you prefer? Why?

## Step 2

Create an outline for your response.

_____

**First reason:**
_____
_____
_____

**Second reason:**
_____
_____
_____

**Like because:** _____

**Think that:** _____

## Step 3

Write a response using your outline from above.

I prefer to travel by _____.
I like traveling by _____ because _____
_____.
I like to travel by _____ because _____.
In addition, I like _____.
Traveling by _____ is my favorite way to travel
because _____.

### Extension

**Work with a partner. Take turns saying your response. Then change partners two more times. Time yourselves!**

Your time: _____ seconds        Partner one's time: _____ seconds
Your time: _____ seconds        Partner two's time: _____ seconds
Your time: _____ seconds        Partner three's time: _____ seconds

# Integrated

## Getting Ready to Speak

### A. Learn the words.

**Key Vocabulary**

| | |
|---|---|
| appear | to be seen |
| earn | to make money by working |
| disappoint | to not meet expectations |

**TOEFL Vocabulary**

| | |
|---|---|
| course load | the number of courses taken by a student |
| extra-curricular | after school; non-academic |
| audition | a trial performance for an actor |
| on the other hand | but |
| degree | educational qualification |

**B. Listen to the first part of a conversation. Then answer the questions.** `Track 69`

1. What are the students discussing?
   The students are discussing _____.

2. What reasons does the student give for having difficulty choosing his courses?
   The student _____.

3. What do you think the student should do?
   The student _____.

**Now practice the questions and answers with a partner.**

**C. Listen and repeat.** `Track 70`

# Practice

○ A. **Listen to the full conversation and take notes.** [Track 71]

| Man | Woman |
|---|---|
| • Choosing _____ | • That would be _____ |
| • Can't decide if _____ | • What kind of _____ |
| • Maybe _____ | • If more courses, could _____ |
| • A sports club or _____ | _____ |
| • And could start _____ | • Money is not so _____ |
| • And could earn _____ | • If join a club then can _____ |
| • This is a _____ | _____ |
| | and meet _____ |

B. **Use your notes to complete the answers.**

　1. What are some reasons the students discuss for taking a full course load?
　　The students discuss _____.

　2. What are some reasons the students discuss for joining a club?
　　The students discuss _____.

👤👤 **Now practice the questions and answers with a partner.**

C. **Read the prompt.**

> The students discuss two different possibilities. Describe the advantages of each choice. Then state which of the two choices you prefer and why.

## Sample Response and Outline

**D. Listen to the sample response and complete the outline.** (Track 72)

The conversation is about _____.

    A. Take fewer classes and _____

        **1.** Join a _____

        **2.** Do _____

    B. Take many courses

        **1.** finish _____

        **2.** start working and _____

    C. Join a club and _____

        **1.** Have _____

        **2.** Meet _____

Conclusion: I think _____
_____.

**E. Write your own conclusion using the outline from above.**

Conclusion: I think he should _____
because _____.

## Speaking Practice

**F. Now work with a partner. Take turns saying your own response using the outline from above.**

Your time: _____ seconds    Your partner's time: _____ seconds

## TOEFL Vocabulary Practice

**G. Fill in the blanks with the correct words.**

| on the other hand | audition | course load | extra-curricular | degree |
|---|---|---|---|---|

**1.** There were over thirty actors at the _____ for the new Steven Spielberg movie.

**2.** It is hard to have free time if you have a heavy _____.

**3.** Sports teams and hobby clubs are some examples of _____ activities at school.

**4.** It usually takes four years to earn a _____ at university.

**5.** I really like that new computer. _____ I don't really need a new one right now.

# Test

## Step 1

Listen to the conversation and take notes. **Track 73**

| Man | Woman |
|---|---|
| • Auditions for the _____ <br> • You should _____ <br> • It would be _____ <br> • It would be _____ <br> • If you join the play you won't _____ <br> _____ | • I want to but _____ <br> • I have to _____ <br> • Final exams _____ <br> _____ <br> • If I don't do well my parents will be <br> _____ <br> • But they also like to _____ <br> • I don't know _____ |

## Step 2

Read the prompt.

> The students are discussing joining a school play. Describe the advantages and disadvantages of joining the school play. Then state if you would join the play and why.

## Step 3

Create an outline for your response.

The conversation is about _____.

    A. Wants to join the play because

        **1.** _____

        **2.** Good _____

        **3.** Parents enjoy _____

    B. Thinks she should study because

        **1.** Get _____

        **2.** Don't _____

        **3.** Can spend time _____

Conclusion: I would prefer _____.

# Step 4

Write a response using your outline.

> The conversation is about _____.
> The female student wants to _____
> because _____
> _____.
> However, she thinks _____
> because _____
> _____.
> I would prefer _____
> because _____.

**Work with a partner. Take turns saying your response. Then change partners two more times. Time Yourselves!**

Your time: _____ seconds        Partner one's time: _____ seconds

Your time: _____ seconds        Partner two's time: _____ seconds

Your time: _____ seconds        Partner three's time: _____ seconds

# Check-up

**Fill in the blanks with the correct words.**

| late | despise | hectic | appearing | disappoint | earn |
|------|---------|--------|-----------|------------|------|

1. Mothers with jobs often have very _____ schedules.

2. Leonardo DiCaprio became a superstar after _____ in *Titanic*.

3. In *Romeo and Juliet*, the Capulet and the Montague families _____ each other.

4. The boss will be angry if you are _____ for work.

5. I want to work hard so that I don't _____ my parents.

6. Many students work during the summer to _____ money for school.

# [ 12 ] Independent

## Getting Ready to Speak

### A. Learn the words.

**Key Vocabulary**

| | |
|---|---|
| **efficient** | well organized |
| **rapidly** | quickly |
| **excess** | too much; extra |

**TOEFL Vocabulary**

| | |
|---|---|
| **source** | origin; place where something begins or comes from |
| **professional** | doing work for pay instead of as a hobby |
| **vast** | huge in size or amount |
| **data** | facts or information |
| **topic** | subject |

### B. Read the prompt. Then answer the questions.

Talk about what you do on the Internet.

**1.** What do you like to do on the Internet?
   I like to _____.

**2.** How long do you spend on the Internet?
   I spend _____ on the Internet.

**3.** When do you use the Internet?
   I use the Internet _____.

**Now practice the questions and answers with a partner.**

**C. Listen and repeat.** Track 74

# Practice

Prompt 1

**A. Read the prompt. Then take turns answering the questions with a partner.**

Talk about your favorite website.

1. What is your favorite website?
2. Why is this your favorite website?
3. Do you trust what you read on this website? Why?
4. Why do you think this is a good website?

**B. Make a list of Internet words and phrases with your classmates.**

_____

_____

_____

_____

Prompt 2

**C. Read the prompt. Then complete the answers with your own information.**

How do you get information for school projects?

What?      I usually have to do research for _____.

Where?     I usually _____ to get information.

How long?  It usually takes _____ to find the information I need.

Why?       I use _____ because _____.

**Now practice your answers with a partner.**

**D. Make a list of research words and phrases with a partner.**

_____

_____

_____

_____

**E. Read the prompt. Then underline the phrases you could use in your own response.**

> People use the Internet to find out information on many topics and for both professional research and general information. Do you think the Internet is a good source of information? Why?

**Reasons for and against using the Internet for research**

- unreliable
- can be changed easily
- many points of view
- not everything available
- easy to use
- ideas are stolen from others

## Sample Response and Outline

**F. Listen to the sample responses and complete the outlines.** [Track 75]

**Sample response 1**

_____

**First reason:**
_____
_____
_____

**Second reason:**
_____
_____

**Think this because:**
_____
_____

**Think that:** _____
_____

**Sample response 2**

_____

**First reason:**
_____
_____
_____

**Second reason:**
_____
_____

**Think this because:**
_____
_____

**Think that:** _____
_____

## TOEFL Vocabulary Practice

**G. Fill in the blanks with the correct words.**

| topic | vast | source | professional | data |
|-------|------|--------|--------------|------|

1. Oranges are an excellent _____ of vitamin C.
2. _____ soccer players can make a lot of money.
3. Computers can manage _____ at very high speeds.
4. The Pacific Ocean is a _____ body of water between Asia and the Americas.
5. The teacher assigned the writing _____ to the students.

# Test

## Step 1

Read the prompt.

> People use the Internet to find out information on many topics and for both professional research and general information. Do you think the Internet is a good source of information? Why?

## Step 2

Create an outline for your response.

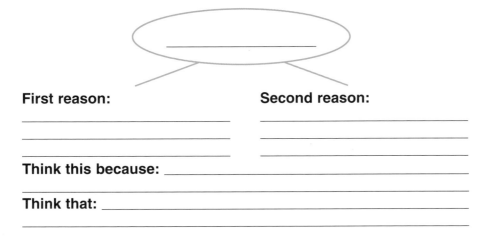

**First reason:**

_____

_____

_____

**Second reason:**

_____

_____

_____

**Think this because:** _____

_____

**Think that:** _____

_____

## Step 3

Write a response using your outline from above.

I think the Internet is _____.

The Internet is _____.

People can _____.

The information on the Internet is _____

_____.

The Internet is good/bad for research because _____

_____.

**Extension**

👤👤 **Work with a partner. Take turns saying your response. Then change partners two more times. Time yourselves!**

Your time: _____ seconds          Partner one's time: _____ seconds

Your time: _____ seconds          Partner two's time: _____ seconds

Your time: _____ seconds          Partner three's time: _____ seconds

# Integrated

## Getting Ready to Speak

### A. Learn the words.

**Key Vocabulary**

| | |
|---|---|
| baton | a short, thin stick used by a conductor to direct musicians |
| conductor | director of an orchestra or choir |
| brass | metal made by mixing steel and copper |

**TOEFL Vocabulary**

| | |
|---|---|
| orchestra | large group of classical musicians |
| full-size | being the normal size for its kind |
| group | people who do something together |
| hollow | empty; full of air |
| stretch | to pull something so that it becomes longer |

**B. Listen to the first part of a lecture. Then answer the questions.** Track 76

1. What is the lecture mainly about?
   The lecture is about _____.

2. How many sections does an orchestra have?
   An orchestra has _____.

3. What else do you think the professor will talk about?
   I think the professor will talk about _____.

**Now practice the questions and answers with a partner.**

**C. Listen and repeat.** Track 77

# Practice

## Note-taking

**A. Listen to the full lecture and take notes.** `Track 78`

- Group who plays _____
- Full-size is about one _____
- All play different _____
- Has many groups called _____
- There are four _____
- Instruments made of wood, _____
- Orchestra leader is called the _____
- Uses small stick, called a _____
- Players watch it to see how _____

**B. Use your notes to complete the answers.**

**1.** What are the four sections of an orchestra?

The four sections of an orchestra are _____

_____.

**2.** How does a conductor lead the orchestra?

The conductor leads the orchestra with a _____ that shows players

_____ they should play.

**Now practice the questions and answers with a partner.**

## Prompt

**C. Read the prompt.**

The professor discusses orchestras. Using points and examples from the lecture, describe what an orchestra is and what the people in an orchestra do.

**D. Listen to the sample response and complete the outline.** Track 79

The lecture is about _____.

    A. The one hundred players

        **1.** make _____

        **2.** play _____

    B. Orchestra sections

        **1.** _____

        **2.** _____

        **3.** _____

        **4.** _____

    C. The Orchestra leader

        **1.** is called _____

        **2.** knows _____

        **3.** uses a small stick called _____

## Speaking Practice

**E. Now work with a partner. Take turns saying your own response using the outline from above.**

Your time: _____ seconds      Your partner's time: _____ seconds

## TOEFL Vocabulary Practice

**F. Fill in the blanks with the correct words.**

| hollow | orchestra | stretch | group | full-size |
|--------|-----------|---------|-------|-----------|

**1.** Athletes have to _____ their muscles before they play a sport.

**2.** A musician must practice for a long time if he wishes to join an

    _____.

**3.** A _____ whale shark can be up to fifteen meters long.

**4.** The political _____ led by Hitler was called the Nazis.

**5.** A dry coconut is _____ on the inside.

# Test

## Step 1

🎧 **Listen to the lecture and take notes.** `Track 80`

- String section is _____
- String instruments are violins, _____, cellos, double basses, and _____
- Instruments made of _____
- Strings are made of _____ or nylon and _____
- Players pull long sticks called _____
- Bows are made of _____
- The piano is a _____
- It has small strings and _____
- Sound is made when a hammer hits a _____

## Step 2

**Read the prompt.**

> The professor describes the instruments in the string section. Using points and examples from the lecture, name key string instruments and describe how they make sound.

## Step 3

**Create an outline for your response.**

The lecture is about _____ in the orchestra.

  A. String instruments

    **1.** _____

    **2.** _____

    **3.** _____

    **4.** _____

    **5.** _____

  B. They

    **1.** are made of wood

    **2.** are hollow _____

    **3.** have strings of steel or _____

  C. Sound is made with a bow pulled _____

  D. Piano

    **1.** has _____

    **2.** hammers hit _____

## Step 4

Write a response using your outline.

The lecture is about _____.
The five string instruments are _____.
They are made of _____
_____.
Sound is made _____
_____.
A piece is also a string instrument. Sound is made when _____
_____.

Work with a partner. Take turns saying your response. Then change partners two more times. Time yourselves!

Your time: _____ seconds        Partner one's time: _____ seconds
Your time: _____ seconds        Partner two's time: _____ seconds
Your time: _____ seconds        Partner three's time: _____ seconds

# Check-up

**Fill in the blanks with the correct words.**

| efficient | rapidly | excess | baton | conductor | brass |
|-----------|---------|--------|-------|-----------|-------|

1. Many old churches have bells made of _____.
2. John Williams is a world-famous orchestra _____.
3. _____ glue can be a problem when building a model.
4. Airplanes allow people to travel _____ between continents.
5. The _____ used to direct an orchestra is a short, thin stick.
6. A good chef runs a very _____ kitchen.

# [ Review 2 ]

## Step 1

Read the prompt.

> Some people like to celebrate their birthday at home. Other people like to celebrate their birthday at a restaurant. What do you prefer? Why?

## Step 2

Create an outline for your response.

_____

**First reason:**

_____

_____

**Like to:**

_____

_____

**I prefer:** _____

_____

**Second reason:**

_____

_____

_____

_____

## Step 3

Write a response using your outline from above.

I think it is best to celebrate a birthday _____.
I would like to celebrate my birthday by _____
_____.
I think this is the best way to celebrate because _____
_____.

### Extension

**Work with a partner. Take turns saying your response. Then change partners two more times. Time yourselves!**

Your time: _____ seconds        Partner one's time: _____ seconds

Your time: _____ seconds        Partner two's time: _____ seconds

Your time: _____ seconds        Partner three's time: _____ seconds

# Step 1

Read the passage.

> ### Deserts and Forests
> The largest desert in the world is the Sahara Desert. It is located in North Africa. The largest rainforest is the Amazon Jungle. It is located in South America. Forests provide a lot of the world's oxygen. Many forests are being cut down. The trees are used for fuel and wood products.

# Step 2

Listen to the lecture and take notes. Track 81

**Deserts**

- There are _____
- They have very little _____
- Animals' main water sources are _____

**Forests**

- There are _____
- They have a lot of water _____
- They are usually _____

**Forests and deserts**

- A lot more plants and animals _____
- There is more water in the _____

# Step 3

Read the prompt.

The professor talks about forests and deserts. Explain why more animals and plants survive in the forest than in the desert.

## Step 4

Create an outline for your response.

The passage and lecture are about _____.

    A. Deserts

        **1.** There are _____

        **2.** The largest one is _____

        **3.** Animals need little _____

    B. Forests

        **1.** The largest rainforest is the _____

        **2.** Forests _____

        **3.** There are _____

        **4.** There is more _____

## Step 5

Write a response using your outline.

> The passage and lecture were about _____.
> There are _____ of deserts.
> The largest desert is _____.
> Animals need little _____ in the desert.
> The largest rainforest is the _____.
> Many rainforests are being _____.
> However, there are _____.
> because _____.

---

**Extension**

👥 **Work with a partner. Take turns saying your response. Then change partners two more times. Time yourselves!**

Your time: _____ seconds      Partner one's time: _____ seconds

Your time: _____ seconds      Partner two's time: _____ seconds

Your time: _____ seconds      Partner three's time: _____ seconds

## Step 1

Listen to the conversation and take notes. Track 82

| Female student | Male student |
|---|---|
| • Ready for _____<br>• Options?<br>• Why take only _____<br>• Take a few then get _____<br>_____ | • Needs to choose _____<br>• Take a lot of classes or _____<br>_____<br>• Take a few classes then can _____<br>_____<br>• Take many classes then can _____<br>_____<br>• Wants to take art and _____<br>• Could finish school _____<br>• Doesn't know _____ |

## Step 2

Read the prompt.

> The students are discussing what classes the male student should take. Describe the advantages and disadvantages of taking either a lot of classes or taking a few classes. Then state what you would prefer.

## Step 3

Create an outline for your response.

The conversation is about _____.

    A.  The student must choose whether _____

    B.  Take a lot of classes

        **1.**  Can finish _____

        **2.**  Can take classes he _____

    C.  Take a few classes

        **1.**  Can get _____

        **2.**  Make _____

        **3.**  _____

Conclusion: I would prefer _____

_____.

## Step 4

Write a response using your outline.

The conversation is about _____
_____ .
The student must choose _____
_____ .
If he takes a lot of _____
_____ .
If he only takes _____
_____ .
I would prefer _____
_____ .

**Extension**

**Work with a partner. Take turns saying your response. Then change partners two more times. Time yourselves!**

Your time: _____ seconds        Partner one's time: _____ seconds
Your time: _____ seconds        Partner two's time: _____ seconds
Your time: _____ seconds        Partner three's time: _____ seconds

## Step 1

Read the prompt.

> Some students take a course load with lots of different subjects and some students take a course load with subjects mainly in one area, like math or art. What do you think is better? Why?

## Step 2

Create an outline for your response.

_____

**First reason:**

_____

_____

**Better because:**

_____

_____

**Second reason:**

_____

_____

_____

_____

**I think that:** _____

_____

## Step 3

Write a response using your outline from above.

I think students should _____
_____.
Students usually find it _____
because _____.
I think it is better to _____
because _____.

Extension

**Work with a partner. Take turns saying your response. Then change partners two more times. Time yourselves!**

| | |
|---|---|
| Your time: _____ seconds | Partner one's time: _____ seconds |
| Your time: _____ seconds | Partner two's time: _____ seconds |
| Your time: _____ seconds | Partner three's time: _____ seconds |

# Speaking Feedback and Evaluation Form

| The response... | 0 | 1 | 2 | 3 | 4 |
|---|---|---|---|---|---|
| **C O N T E N T** addresses the question or prompt well | | | | | |
| has relevant details | | | | | |
| connects ideas clearly | | | | | |
| **L A N G U A G E** uses accurate grammar | | | | | |
| uses appropriate vocabulary | | | | | |
| has fluent speech | | | | | |
| has clear pronunciation | | | | | |

**Total:** _____ /28

# Basic Skills for the
# TOEFL® iBT 1

Edaan Getzel
Tanya Yaunish

*Speaking*

## Transcript & Answer Key

# Transcript

## [ Unit 1 ]

### Independent

**Page 15**

**C**

M: I wake up at 8 o'clock. For fun, I watch TV at night, and after school, I eat dinner and go to piano class.

**Page 17**

**F**

Sample response 1

M: I love weekends much more than weekdays. During the week, I have to be serious and academic. On the weekend, I like to relax. I deserve a break because I work hard all week at school. Plus, the weekend gives me time to watch a movie or do other things that I enjoy. I love my weekends.

Sample response 2

W: I prefer weekdays to the weekend. I feel that the weekend wastes time, and is so dull. I like to go to school during the week. Being a student is like my job, and I like to do my job well. I also like contributing my thoughts and ideas at school. I also get to see my friends when I'm there. On weekends I do nothing. The weekends are great for some people, but not for me.

### Integrated

**Page 19**

**C**

W: The announcement says that the library will change its hours and now stay open for twenty-four hours a day, seven days a week. This is so students can prepare for their exams. I think the conversation will be about how the change of hours will help the students.

**Page 20**

**B**

W: What's wrong?
M: I've got an essay to write for tomorrow and the library is going to close soon.
W: No, it's not. This is the first day of the new hours.
M: What new hours?
W: Didn't you read the announcement? For the final month of classes, the library will be open twenty-four hours a day.
M: Really? That's fantastic! I was having trouble getting all my work done in the old opening hours. Is it open on Sundays?
W: Yes. Seven days a week.
M: What a great idea! Now I will have enough time to study.
W: I always study at home so it won't make any difference to me.
M: For me it's great because I can't study at home. It's too noisy there. That's why I do everything at the library. Now I have plenty of time to finish this essay. And then it will be easier to study for exams. I think this will help many people.

**Page 21**

**D**

W: The man thinks that the change in library hours is a great idea because it will give him more time to finish his essay and to study for exams. The man can't study at home because it is too noisy, so he does everything in the library. He thinks the longer hours will help many people.

**Page 22**

**Step 2**

M: I hear the university is changing the hours at the computer lab.

W: Don't remind me.

M: What? I think it's a great idea. I always have trouble accessing a computer, especially around final exams. I think this will help.

W: I don't think it will make much difference. They need to get more computers.

M: Yeah, that would be best. But changing the hours will help! Why are you so against it?

W: I work there. Now I will have to get up really early in the morning. And I doubt very many students will go there at 7 a.m.!

M: Oh, I hadn't thought of that. Maybe it won't be permanent and surely they'll pay you more?

W: It sounds like it is permanent. But you're right; they will be paying the workers more. However, I think they should use that money to buy more computers instead. Then many students could use computers at the same time and not have to come in early.

M: That's a good point.

# [ Unit 2 ]

## Independent

**Page 25**

**C**

W: My best friend's name is Kathy. I met her when my family moved to a new apartment two years ago. We like to play computer games together.

**Page 27**

**F**

Sample response 1

W: I think that best friends usually have opposite personalities and like different things. A good example is my best friend and me. I am quiet and my pastimes are usually indoor activities. My friend is very adventurous and likes to do things outdoors. I think we are friends because we find each other interesting.

Sample response 2

M: I think that best friends usually have similar personalities and like the same things. A good example is my best friend and me. We are both adventurous and very outgoing. We both like to do outdoor activities and love to play soccer together. I think we are friends because we have fun together.

## Integrated

**Page 29**

**C**

M: The passage is about Impressionism, which was popular in the 1800s and was started in France. Impressionists painted their experiences, nature, and the outdoors. They often painted trees and lakes. I think the lecture will be about Impressionist painters and their style.

**Page 30**

**B**

W: Impressionists painted things to make them look real. They did this in many ways. In the 19th century, art supplies were light and easy to carry. So, many artists painted nature outdoors. For example, Monet painted in a garden. He dug a hole and put his canvas in it. There he made a painting of young women. He liked painting outside. He told people that he did not have a real studio. However, things in nature often change or move. So, speed was important so that drawings and paintings could be finished quickly. Often they were finished in one or two hours. Sometimes it was faster. Artists like Monet also tried different colors. Some things were very hard to copy. They used red, yellow, and green for sunny paintings. Cloudy scenes used gray and blue. This way they could show how they saw the world.

**Page 31**

**D**

M: The lecture and passage were about Monet and Impressionism. Impressionists liked to paint things in nature such as trees, lakes, or people who were outside. To do this, they painted while outside. Monet also liked to paint outside, so he painted in a garden. He didn't have a real studio. Monet and other Impressionists painted quickly and used many different colors to show how they saw the world. Everything Monet did was very normal for Impressionists.

**Page 32**

**Step 2**

M: Berthe Morisot studied drawing as a child with her three sisters. She began by drawing and painting outdoor scenes. After, she painted scenes from her home. Her parents were happy that she was an artist. Her sisters and their children were her models. Later, she had her own style. Her unique style was very feminine. No matter what medium she used, she used light brush strokes. Critics really liked her work because it was realistic. She often painted in nature. She liked to paint trees, ponds, and lakes. She didn't like painting crowds of busy people. In her paintings there are usually one or two people with water and leaves. Often, the people are resting or boating on a lake. She sometimes painted while sitting in a boat. It was difficult because the boats moved. Once, she became angry and threw her painting into the lake. She died in 1895, at age 54.

# [ Unit 3 ]

**Independent**

**Page 35**

**C**

M: I use a cell phone to make my phone calls. I use it all the time. However, I hate to send text messages.

**Page 37**

**F**

Sample response 1
M: I prefer to communicate with old-fashioned telephones. I don't understand new technology. Computers are very complicated, and cell phones get really bad reception. Telephones, however, are really easy to use, very dependable and you can find them everywhere. For me, telephones are the best way to communicate.

Sample response 2
W: I love to talk to people through instant messaging. It is so fast and easy that anyone can use it. In addition, I can have multiple conversations at one time and send files. All my friends use it and we all have a custom of coming home from school and chatting online until dinner time. I love instant messaging.

**Page 39**

**B**

M: So, have you decided where to go for university yet?
W: No, I still haven't decided if I should stay here or move away.
M: What would be good about staying near home?
W: It would be cheaper because I could live with my parents.

**C**

W: The students are discussing if the woman should study in her hometown or move to another city. The woman says that if she stays at home, it will be cheaper and she can live with her parents. I think the rest of the conversation will be about why she should move away.

**Page 40**

**A**

M: So, have you decided where to go for university yet?
W: No, I still haven't decided if I should stay here or move away.
M: What would be good about staying near home?
W: It would be cheaper because I could live with my parents. And I wouldn't have to fly home for the holidays. Plus I know this city really well and I have a lot of friends here.
M: So, why would you like to move away?
W: It would be nice to see a new city. I would be motivated to meet new people. Also, I'd like to become more independent. My parents aren't very flexible with what they let me do.
M: Yes, that's a difficult decision. If you move you would have more freedom, but you wouldn't see your family and friends often. And if you stay you won't have to be responsible for everything but you would miss out on doing new things. Do you have to decide immediately?
W: No, I have time to think about it some more.

**Page 41**

**D**

W: The conversation is about whether the student should stay at home or move away for university. The advantages of living at home are that it's cheaper because she could live with her parents and that she wouldn't have to fly home for the holidays. She also knows the city well and has many friends there. However, there are advantages to living away from home as well. For example, she could see a new city and therefore meet new people. She would also become more independent, and so have a more flexible lifestyle. I think she should stay at home, as she will be more comfortable there and she won't miss her friends or family. I think family and friends are more important.

**Page 42**

**Step 1**

W: Hi John, how is your online course?
M: Good. Why do you ask?
W: Well, I'm thinking about doing an online course. Could you give me some advice?
M: Sure. You have to be motivated to complete an online course. Most of it is independent study, so you must make yourself a schedule. Also, you have to be responsible enough to solve problems by yourself.
W: Aren't there professors to help you?
M: Yes, but it's different from a classroom. In a classroom, the professor can give you some guidance immediately. For an online course, you have to email the professor.
W: What do you like about the course?
M: It's really flexible. I have the freedom to study when I want to. I can have a job at the same time. Also I don't have to move away to go to school. That makes it cheaper. An online degree is great for some people but not for others.
W: Thanks for explaining it. I will need to decide if it would be good for me.

# [ Unit 4 ]

**Independent**

**Page 45**

**C**

W: I live in a big house. Near my house, there are a lot of parks and walking trails. The best thing about my home is the beautiful view of the mountains from our backyard.

**Page 47**

**F**

Sample response 1

W: I think that living in the city has many more advantages than living in the countryside. The city is so much fun. Fun things in the city include sports games, museums, and movie theaters. The countryside doesn't have these things. Moreover, the city is so convenient because shops are close. Living in the countryside has too many disadvantages.

Sample response 2

M: I think that the countryside has more advantages than the city. The countryside, unlike the city, has a lot of space. This is good for kids who want to play. Also, the countryside is healthier because it has much cleaner air compared to the city. The countryside is a much better place to live than the city.

**Integrated**

**Page 49**

**B**

M: There are many different animals that live in the Arctic. Some live on land and some in the sea. The most famous Arctic animal is the polar bear. It is land dwelling.

**C**

M: The lecture is about Arctic animals. The most famous Arctic animal is the polar bear. I think the professor will talk about other Arctic animals.

**Page 50**

**A**

M: There are many different animals that live in the Arctic. Some live on land and some in the sea. The most famous Arctic animal is the polar bear. It is land-dwelling. So are the caribou and the arctic hare. The caribou is a kind of deer. Its babies are born on the tundra. They can walk at one day old. The arctic hare is like a rabbit. They live in herds with hundreds of other hares. In the sea there are whales, seals, and walrus. Famous Arctic whales are the beluga and the narwhal. The male narwhal has a long tusk. You can also find birds in the far north. Most of these are sea birds. Some stay in the Arctic all year and some migrate south in the winter. They eat plants and fish. All of these animals have adapted to living in the cold and have developed ways to avoid their enemies.

**Page 51**

**D**

W: The lecture is about different Arctic animals. There are many land and sea animals in the Arctic. For example, the land animals called polar bears are the most famous Arctic animal. There are also caribou, which are like deer. Its babies can walk at a day old! And arctic hares, which are like rabbits, live in herds. There are many sea animals, such as whales, seals, and walruses. One type of whale even has a long tusk. There are many birds in the Arctic. Some stay there all year but some migrate in winter. There are many animals in the Arctic, which shows they can adapt well to their environment.

## Page 52
### Step 1

W: Polar-dwelling animals have to adapt to live in the Arctic. They all eat food that is easy to find. Caribou and musk oxen eat green plants. Arctic foxes and wolves eat other animals. The caribou migrate south to find food and to keep warm in the winter. Musk oxen have special hooves to get grass from under the snow. They also have very long fur to keep warm. Polar bears and whales have a thick layer of fat. This protects them from the cold water. Some animals change color to hide from their enemies. The arctic hare has brown fur in the summer. But, in the winter it has white fur. Many Arctic birds are the same. In the summer they can hide in the brown grass. In the winter they hide in the white snow on the tundra so their enemies can't see them. This is how animals adapt in the Arctic.

# [ Unit 5 ]

## Independent

### Page 55
### C

M: My favorite sport to play is basketball. It is my favorite sport to play because it is such a fast and competitive game. My favorite sport to watch is American football.

### Page 57
### F

Sample response 1
M: I prefer physical activities. Athletic games usually allow more of my friends to participate. This gives me a chance to socialize. Also, I feel great after I run around a little bit. My body feels energized, so I can focus more on my homework. Physical activities are much more fun for me.

Sample response 2
W: I like nonphysical activities. I love to read books and connect with different kinds of characters. When reading books or watching TV, I have to use my brain a lot more, so I feel that it makes me smarter. Plus, I can read books anywhere I go. Because of this, I prefer nonphysical activities.

## Integrated

### Page 59
### C

W: A new study center will open. Computer access and assistance from student tutors will be available. I think the conversation will be about the new study center.

### Page 60
### B

M: Have you heard about the new study center that's going to open next week?
W: Yeah, I heard.
M: Isn't it fantastic? There will be more access to computers.
W: Yes, computers are a great educational aid.
M: Plus, there are going to be student tutors available to help with homework and stuff.
W: Yeah, that's kind of pointless.
M: Pointless? Why would you say that?
W: Because there aren't enough volunteers. Students who frequent the center are going to have to wait a long time to get help. And then they will only have five minutes with the volunteer. Another concern is that helpers are appointed to students needing help randomly. So, if you find a helper you really like, you won't always get the same person.

M: Hmmm...That is a problem. But don't say it's pointless. At least it's a start.

W: I think they should have put the money into a tutoring service instead. If you paid the tutors, you'd get a lot more interest.

## Page 61

### D

M: The conversation is about the services that will be offered at the new study center. The man is happy because there will be more computers there and there will be student tutors available to help with homework. The woman is concerned that the center will be pointless because she knows that there are not enough student volunteers. As such, students will have to wait a long time to see a tutor. Then, once they are appointed a tutor, they will only have five minutes with them. Also, the tutors will be assigned randomly. She suggests that the university should use the money for a tutoring service instead.

## Page 62

### Step 2

M: I can't believe this. They just announced that they're not going to have free tutors anymore.

W: I know. It's just awful, isn't it?

M: Yeah, but if there's no money there's no money. I wouldn't want them to raise student fees either. And you can't expect students to volunteer for free. They're too busy.

W: Well, how about spending a little less money on sports? They don't cut back on the amount of money they give the football team. This is a university. It's supposed to be about education first. Cutting back on educational services before sports is awful. A lot of students need that free service. Now there will be extra work for the professors too. They'll have to have longer office hours to help all the students who need it.

M: Hey, those are good points. You should write to the school paper or something.

W: I think I will.

# [ Unit 6 ]

### Independent

## Page 65

### C

W: I usually buy things to eat and I normally get money from my part time job. In the future, I want to buy a car.

## Page 67

### F

Sample response 1

W: I think that it is better to spend my spare money immediately. I always like to have fun. Concerts and movies are so much fun. I also always like to look fashionable. Fashion styles are always changing, so I always have to buy the most modern clothes. Spending my spare money makes me happy.

Sample response 2

M: I think that it is better to save your money for the future. Saving your money allows you to buy more expensive things. Last year, I bought a new computer. It is also good to have money for an emergency. If I lose something important, I can always replace it. Saving money makes me feel more responsible.

**Page 69**

**C**

M: Astronomy is the study of the universe. Astronomers study the planets and stars in our solar system. I think the lecture will be about astronomy and our solar system.

**Page 70**

**B**

W: Astronomers want to find out more about the solar system. It is the part of the universe we live in. They look at the size of planets and how they orbit the Sun. They use telescopes to study the planets and the Sun because they are very far away. For example, it takes eight minutes for sunlight to reach Earth. The Sun is a star. It is bright because it is closer to us than other stars. We live on a planet called Earth. Our planet is the third one from the Sun. Jupiter is the biggest planet. There are eight planets in our solar system. There used to be nine planets altogether. As of 2006, Pluto is no longer considered a planet. The Earth orbits the Sun once a year. The Earth also has a moon. The moon is covered with craters. The moon orbits the Earth once a month.

**Page 71**

**D**

W: The lecture and passage were about astronomy and the solar system. Astronomers study the universe. They believe that the universe began with an explosion. They look at the size and movement of planets around the Sun. There used to be nine planets, but now there are only eight. They use telescopes to study the planets and the Sun because they are far away. The Sun is bright because it is closer to us than other stars. The planets are spheres like Earth.

**Page 72**

**Step 2**

M: The moon is a natural satellite. It orbits the Earth. It takes a month to go around the Earth. It is the only object in space that people have visited. Man first walked on it in 1969. Altogether, 12 men have been on the moon. You can see it clearly with your eyes, binoculars, or a telescope. We can see a full moon once a month, too. People use telescopes to look at the craters on it. There is no wind or rain on the moon. This means the craters do not go away. It is quite close to us. It is bright because we see sunlight bounce off it. When it goes between us and the Sun it is called an eclipse. We always see the same side of the moon.

# [ Review 1 ]

**Page 76**

**Step 2**

W: I just heard that the school is going to close down the cafeteria.
M: Yeah, what a stupid idea!
W: Well, I didn't really go there anyway. I don't care, I go to the shops.
M: I go every day. What am I supposed to do now?
W: You can leave school at lunch time if you want.
M: But that's not really convenient. I like to sit and study there when I have my lunch. Why didn't the school just stop students from leaving at lunch time? That would be far better. I'm going to tell the school what I think of this rubbish. It's just not realistic!
W: Are you being serious?
M: If I talk to some others, maybe we could influence the decision to close it.
W: I don't think that the school will be too flexible about their decision.
M: Yeah, but I have to try and get them to consider the people that use it every day.

**Page 78**

**Step 1**

W: A business is a company that sells goods or services to people. They do this to make money, which is called profit. They can be very small or very big. A business could be a local shop or a café. Some companies have sites all over the world. It takes time for them to become this good. Most companies start small and become big when they make more profit. This is how the company Google became so popular. It looks for things on the Internet. It organizes the information so it is easy to read. It started in 1998. At the time, its office was in a garage. Slowly it got bigger and bigger. As their technology got better and adapted, it became more popular. Now Google is a very big company that is known all over the world. A company is better when its goods or services are more convenient for you.

# [ Unit 7 ]

**Independent**

**Page 81**

**C**

M: My favorite subject is history. It is my favorite subject because I find history to be so interesting. My least favorite subject is English because I do not really like writing.

**Page 83**

**F**

Sample response 1

M: I am much better at science and math than music and art. I like science and math because I can actually see results. I feel better because when I finish I feel that I achieved a particular goal. Music and art are nice, but they don't have a correct answer. I like to see correct answers, and science and math allow me to get them. I really love science.

Sample response 2

W: I am much better at the humanities subjects than I am at math and science. The humanities subjects allow me to express my feelings. They can also be very inspirational. I like studying the humanities subjects because I am good at them, and they make me feel good. Finally, I like them because everyone can enjoy these subjects.

**Integrated**

**Page 85**

**B**

M: So, what are your plans for summer vacation?
W: I have some responsibilities. I'm going to be working with my dad. What about you?
M: I haven't decided yet. I could go to France with my aunt or I might stay here and visit my grandparents.
W: Well, traveling might be fun. You could experience a whole new culture.

**C**

W: The students are discussing if the male student should go abroad for summer vacation or stay home. The student says that it would be a lot of fun and he would experience a new culture. I think the rest of the conversation will be about what the student could do at home in the vacation and I think the student should go to France and experience French culture.

A

M: So, what are your plans for summer vacation?
W: I have some responsibilities. I'm going to be working with my dad. What about you?
M: I haven't decided yet. I could go to France with my aunt or I might stay here and visit my grandparents.
W: Well, traveling might be fun. You could experience a whole new culture.
M: Yes, it would be really interesting, but it could also be difficult.
W: Really. Why?
M: I don't speak any French.
W: You could learn some.
M: Yes, but I don't have a lot of time. Also, I'd miss my friends. It would be nice to visit all the museums, though.
W: It might also be nice to stay here. You could spend your time relaxing.
M: That's true. It might be a little boring and I won't meet any new people, but I could save a lot of money.
W: You definitely have a difficult decision. Either way your summer will be better than mine.

Page 87

D

M: The conversation is about the students' plans for their summer vacation. The male student has two choices. First, he can travel to France with his aunt. This would be fun because he could experience a new culture and visit some museums. However, he would miss his friends and it might be difficult because he can't speak French. He could also stay home and visit his grandparents. This would be more relaxing and he could save some money. But, it might be a little boring and he wouldn't meet any new people. I think he should travel to France because it's more interesting than staying home. People should spend their youth experiencing new and different things.

Page 88

Step 1

M: Have you found a job yet for your summer vacation? I'm going to work at a summer camp.
W: No, I'm not sure if I want a job this summer or not.
M: Well, I definitely like having the extra money. I'm saving some for tuition. The rest of it I can spend. I'm planning to buy a new cell phone.
W: That sounds great. But I'm still not sure. I like having freedom. I can stay up late with my friends and not worry about going to work.
M: That's true. But, I've also met a lot of great people at my job. We become friends quickly because we have the same interests.
W: I don't know, it sounds like a lot of responsibility. I want to earn money, but I also want to enjoy my youth. I don't know what decision to make.
M: You'd better hurry or you won't find a good job.

# [ Unit 8 ]

**Independent**

Page 91

C

W: I like to watch comedies. I usually watch TV for an hour and a half every day. I watch TV for half an hour in the morning, and an hour at night.

## Page 93

**F**

Sample response 1

W: I think that television is a great influence on children. Television can connect children with so much content. They can see things that they could never see in real life. In addition, TV can send positive messages to kids. This will help them grow up. TV can help kids connect with many different things.

Sample response 2

M: I think that TV is usually a bad influence on children. Many critics think that TV is too violent for children. Kids then copy the violent behavior that they see on TV. In addition, watching a lot of TV can be really unhealthy because it reduces the amount of time that kids go outside to play. TV teaches children bad habits.

## Integrated

## Page 95

**B**

M: Acid rain is rain that contains a lot of sulfur. It also contains nitrogen. Acid rain is formed when coal, oil, or wood are burned. We burn a lot of coal to make electricity. We use electricity in homes and factories. We burn oil to make our cars go and to make airplanes fly. We make fires to keep us warm in winter time. When we do these things, we are releasing sulfur and nitrogen gases into the air.

**C**

M: The lecture is about acid rain. Acid rain contains sulfur and nitrogen. It is formed when coal, oil, or wood are burned. I think the professor will talk about ways to reduce acid rain.

## Page 96

**A**

M: Acid rain is rain that contains a lot of sulfur. It also contains nitrogen. Acid rain is formed when coal, oil, or wood are burned. We burn a lot of coal to make electricity. We use electricity in homes and factories. We burn oil to make our cars go and to make airplanes fly. We make fires to keep us warm in winter time. When we do these things, we are releasing sulfur and nitrogen gases into the air. These gases float into the sky. Then they float into the clouds. Then they mix with water drops inside the clouds. When there is a lot of water inside a cloud, it will begin to rain. This kind of rain is very dangerous. It can cause a lot of damage to nature. The acid in the rain is bad for plants. It is bad for animals. It can kill them. It can even cause damage to the structure of some buildings. Acid rain is a big problem all over the world.

## Page 97

**D**

W: The lecture is about acid rain, which contains sulfur and nitrogen. It forms when we burn oil, coal, or wood. We do this to make electricity for homes and factories, to make cars go and airplanes fly, and to keep us warm. Burning releases sulfur and nitrogen gases. They float into the sky and into clouds where they mix with water drops. Clouds then release acid rain that is dangerous. It can kill plants and animals and damage buildings. It is a big problem for the whole world.

## Page 98

**Step 1**

W: Acid rain does a lot of harm. It can damage buildings made of sandstone or limestone. The acid rain burns the buildings. It makes small holes in them. This damages the structure of buildings. In time they become weaker. Acid rain falls into lakes and rivers. It hurts the plants and animals that live in the water. The acid burns the animals. The acid also kills the insects that water animals feed on. The acid kills fish eggs. It kills fish too. If birds eat dead fish, they can also get sick. In some parts of the world there are big lakes with no animal life in them. All the animals have died because of acid rain. Acid rain falls on forests. It damages the leaves of trees. It runs down into the soil. It makes the soil too acidic. Then plants can no longer grow in the soil. Something must be done to stop this.

# [ Unit 9 ]

## Independent

**Page 101**

**C**

M: I need to be in a quiet environment when I am studying. I like to drink coffee while studying and I prefer to study late at night.

**Page 103**

**F**

Sample response 1

M: I hate doing homework. I'd much rather be playing with my friends. Homework isn't very useful. I have managed to get really good grades without doing much homework. I comprehend what my teacher says the first time, so I shouldn't have to spend more time at home doing it again.

Sample response 2

W: I like doing my homework. I need repetition and routine to be a good student and to understand what I have learned. Homework also helps by teaching me discipline that I'll need later on. Homework is vital to my future success and I enjoy the challenge of it. As a result, I'm happy to do it.

## Integrated

**Page 105**

**C**

W: The Health Sciences Department will increase professors' office hours. Students should ask their professors to tell them their new hours. I think the conversation will be about the announcement to change professors' office hours.

**Page 106**

**B**

M: Oh! This is an unexpected surprise!
W: What? What's going on?
M: Did you see this announcement? The professors are increasing their office hours.
W: Really? All over campus?
M: No, just in the Health Sciences Department. There's not enough demand in the other departments yet.
W: Oh. That doesn't help me. I'm a business major.
M: Well, for me it's great. Right now, my professor's office hours conflict with my schedule.
W: What's the problem?
M: I always have class during them. I thought I was just unlucky, but I guess a lot of students are having the same problem.
W: So, do the new hours work better with your timetable?
M: I don't know. I have to ask the professors for their new office hours.
W: Oh, didn't they inform you?
M: No. I'll have to go to class and then I can ask them.
W: Well, it's good that they have responded to the students' needs. I hope it works out for you.
M: Me too. There are a few classes I really need help with if I hope to advance next year.

D

M: The conversation is about the increase in office hours for professors in the Health Sciences Department. The man thinks the new office hours are great. Right now, he cannot see his professors during their office hours because he always has class at that time. He is having trouble in some classes so he needs to be able to spend time with his professors. A lot of other students are having the same problem too. He needs to get extra help with some of his classes during the new office hours. He is therefore very happy with the announcement.

Step 2

M: Do you want to form a study group with some of the others in our sociology class?
W: That sounds like a great idea. We can get together and discuss our class work.
M: Great. Where should we meet?
W: Didn't you hear? Because of the demand, the library has dedicated certain rooms to be used for group study.
M: Really? That's wonderful!
W: I know.
M: I am part of a literature study group, and we usually have to meet at the cafeteria because there's nowhere else to meet. The problem there is that it can get pretty noisy.
W: Right, but you don't want to go anywhere too quiet for discussions, because you might bother other people.
M: Exactly. But this is great. Can you reserve a room every week?
W: Sure, if I inform the library that we need the room.
M: Great. Let's go to the library before class and reserve one. Then we can ask if anyone wants to join our group when we go to class.
W: Sounds good.

# [ Unit 10 ]

## Independent

C

W: I like gym class because I can run around with my friends. My favorite part of gym class is when we play dodge ball. My least favorite part of gym class is when the teacher tells us to go back to class.

F

Sample response 1
W: Physical education should be a necessity in school. Exercise is important to maintain a balanced and healthy lifestyle. Nowadays, there are many overweight children. P.E. is a great way to make kids exercise, and it can teach them important habits to have as an adult. P.E. helps kids now as well as in the future.

Sample response 2
M: With the increasing number of students falling behind in school, I suggest making P.E. an optional subject. The typical student needs to spend more time studying. In addition, there are many places to play sports after school. Using school time for this is a waste of time and money. P.E. is important, but it shouldn't be in school.

## Integrated

C

M: People can watch television and listen to the radio all over the world now. People used to read, tell stories, play music, or go to the theater. I think the lecture will be about technology and entertainment.

# Transcript

## Page 116

### B

W: Currently, technology has a huge effect on our lives. Years ago, people were limited with what they could do. Now we have many choices. We can watch a movie without going to the theater or listen to music without going to a concert. We use the TV, radio, or computer to have fun. We can do this just by pressing a button on a remote control. You can even use technology away from home. Anyone can play with their phone or listen to music when they go outside. These changes were gradual to begin with, but recent progress has been fast. You can even watch some TV channels on your phone. It's easy for us to have fun in our homes now. And we have more time for fun because we don't have to go out. We can do what we want, when we want. We have more choice now.

## Page 117

### D

W: The lecture and passage were about technology in entertainment. It has a huge effect on the way we relax. In the past people used to read books, tell stories, or go to the theater for fun. Now we also watch TV, listen to the radio, and play on the computer. Because of remote controls, it is very easy to do these things. We can even do these things outside now. Things are changing quickly these days. Because of technology, we can do more things more easily.

## Page 118

### Step 2

W: Television is a huge part of entertainment. It lets us see moving pictures and hear sounds at the same time. To begin with, there were only a few channels. TVs were small and the pictures were in black and white. In 1963, TV was first shown in full color. As technology moves on, televisions get bigger and better. With cable television we can watch and record hundreds of channels. You can even choose what each channel will show. People can also buy movies and programs on disc. They can watch them on their TV. You can do lots of different things with your TV. You can play music, DVDs, or even video games on your TV now. This gives people more choice of things to do. In the future, you will be able to do even more with your TV.

# [ Unit 11 ]

**Independent**

## Page 121

### C

M: I dislike how slow traveling by land is. An advantage of traveling by sea is that it is usually cheaper. An advantage of traveling by land is that you can stop when you need to.

## Page 123

### F

Sample response 1

M: I prefer to travel in my car. I am very independent, and my car gives me freedom. But mostly, I despise going to the airport because it is so hectic. To fly you are supposed to be there 90 minutes early, and if you are late, you miss your flight. In addition, the airport is not always located near your home. So, I will always drive my car.

Sample response 2

W: Flying is my preferred mode of transport. It's great because it requires no effort. I don't have to worry about anything. I can just sit in my seat and fall asleep and when I wake up, I'm in a new city. It's fast and easy, so I love to fly.

## Page 125

**B**

W: What are you doing?
M: I'm deciding which classes to take next semester. It's really difficult.
W: It is? Why?
M: Because I can't decide if I should take a full course load or not.
W: What will you do if you don't take all your classes?
M: Well, I could join an extra-curricular activity.

**C**

W: The students are discussing which classes to take next semester. The student can't decide if he should take a full course load or not. The student should take a full course load so that he finishes sooner.

## Page 126

**A**

W: What are you doing?
M: I'm deciding which classes to take next semester. It's really difficult.
W: It is? Why?
M: Because I can't decide if I should take a full course load or not.
W: What will you do if you don't take all your classes?
M: Well, I could join an extra-curricular activity.
W: That would be fun. University is about more than just academics. What kind of club would you join?
M: I don't know. I could join a sports club or maybe the drama club. They are having auditions next week.
W: It would be exciting to appear in a play. On the other hand, if you choose to do more courses you could finish your degree faster.
M: Yes, then I can start working sooner and earn some money.
W: Money is not the only important thing, though. If you join a club you can have different experiences and meet lots of new people. You'll be disappointed later if you don't enjoy yourself a little now.
M: This is a hard decision.

## Page 127

**D**

M: The conversation is about how many classes the man should take. He could take fewer classes and do an extra-curricular activity. The man may join a sports club or he may do some volunteer work. If he takes many courses he can finish his degree faster. Then he could start working and earning money. However, if he joins a club, he will have more fun. He could also have some interesting experiences and meet new people. I think he should join a club because studying is not the only important thing. He should also have fun at university.

## Page 128

**Step 1**

M: Hi Lisa. Have you heard the news? They are having auditions for the school play. You should try out. You're such a good actress.
W: I really want to join the school play. But, I don't know if I have time for extra-curricular activities right now.
M: Really? Why not?
W: I have a pretty heavy course load and final exams are coming soon. I want to get good grades, so I have to study hard.
M: Yes, but appearing in the play would be fun. Also, it would be good experience for your Fine Arts degree.
W: I agree with you about that. However, if I do poorly on my exams my parents will be so disappointed. They worked hard to earn my tuition. On the other hand, they do love to watch me act.

M: It might be hard to do both. You won't be able to spend time with your friends if you join the play.

W: Yes, I don't know what I'll do.

# [ Unit 12 ]

## Independent

**Page 131**

**C**

W: I like to play online games. I spend about an hour every day on the Internet after school.

**Page 133**

**F**

Sample response 1

W: The Internet is a great source of important information. Many professional researchers use the Internet because it is the most efficient way to get information. People can get answers to questions rapidly instead of driving to the library. Also, the Internet has much more information than even the biggest library. It's vast and fast, so the Internet is good for research.

Sample response 2

M: The Internet isn't always a good place for research. The information is hard to control. Since anyone can write whatever they want on the Internet, we can't be sure that it is a reliable source of information. Also, due to excess data, it can be hard to find information on a very specific topic. The Internet is great, but isn't always good for research.

## Integrated

**Page 135**

**B**

M: A large group of people who play music together is called an orchestra. A full-size orchestra has about one hundred players. They all play different instruments. They make beautiful music. An orchestra has many groups. Each group plays different instruments. These groups are called "sections." There are four big sections.

**C**

M: The lecture is about orchestras. An orchestra has four sections. I think the professor will talk about what the different sections in an orchestra do.

**Page 136**

**A**

M: A large group of people who play music together is called an orchestra. A full-size orchestra has about one hundred players. They all play different instruments. They make beautiful music. An orchestra has many groups. Each group plays different instruments. These groups are called "sections." There are four big sections. One section is for instruments made out of wood. One is for instruments made out of brass. Another is for drums. The last one is called the string section. The stringed instruments have strings stretched over hollow instruments made of wood. A violin is an example of a stringed instrument. The person who leads the orchestra is called a conductor. He knows the music very well. He knows what all the players have to do. He uses a small stick to show players what to do. The stick is called a baton. Players watch the baton. It shows them how quickly or how slowly they should play.

**Page 137**

**D**

W: An orchestra is a group of players that make music together. There are about one hundred players in a full-size orchestra. They make beautiful music and all play different instruments. There are four different sections in an orchestra. They are the wood, brass, drum, and string sections. The orchestra leader is called the conductor. He knows the music well. He uses a baton to show players what to do. He shows players how quickly or slowly they should play.

**Page 138**

**Step 1**

W: The string section is the biggest group in the orchestra. Members of the string section play violins, violas, cellos, double basses, and pianos. Double basses are like very big violins. They make a deep sound. All the stringed instruments are made of wood and are hollow inside. They have strings on them. The strings are made of steel or nylon. The strings are stretched over holes. Players pull long sticks over the strings to make sound. If they pull slowly, the sounds are sad. If they pull quickly, the sounds are happy. The long stick they use is called a bow. The bow is made of horsehair. A piano is also a string instrument. Many people do not know this. A piano has small strings and hammers inside it. When a player hits a piano key it makes a sound. The sound is made by a hammer hitting a string.

# [ Review 2 ]

**Integrated 1**

**Page 142**

**Step 2**

M: Forests and deserts together cover almost half of the Earth's surface. There are four major types of deserts. There are three types of forests. The plants and animals in the desert have to be able to live on little water. The animals' main water sources are seeds and roots. Forests are the opposite of deserts. The forests get plenty of water. Forests are usually damp and often the air is cool. A lot more plants and animals live in the forest than in the desert. There is more water for animals and plants in the forest than in the desert.

**Integrated 2**

**Page 144**

**Step 1**

W: Nick, are you ready for school to start?
M: Not yet. I need to choose my classes.
W: What are your options?
M: I need to choose if I want to take a lot of classes or just a few classes.
W: Why would you only take a few?
M: If I take a few classes, I could get a job as well. But if I take many classes, I could finish school quicker.
W: Hmm. Do you know what classes you want to take?
M: Yeah there are art and math classes I really want to take and they won't be available next year. And if I take them all then it will be hard work but then I would be finished school this year.
W: But if you only take a few, you could get a job to make money and relax a little.
M: Yeah. I just don't know what to do.
W: Well, good luck deciding!

# Answer Key

## [ Unit 1 ]

**Independent**

### Page 15

**B**

1. I wake up at <u>eight o'clock</u>.
2. For fun, I <u>watch TV at night</u>.
3. After school, I <u>eat dinner and go to piano class</u>.

### Page 16

**A**

1. I often go to my grandmother's house on the weekend.
2. We often go out for dinner on the weekend.
3. My family goes skiing on weekends in winter.
4. Yes. We eat a big family dinner on the weekend.

**B**

Go to church
Eat with my family
Go to football games
Watch a movie

Go out for dinner
Sleep at my friend's house
Go to my grandparents' house
Play computer games

**C**

During the week, I <u>practice tae kwon do</u>.
On the weekend, I <u>play soccer</u>.
During the week, I go to bed at <u>ten thirty</u>.
On the weekend, I go to bed at <u>eleven thirty</u>.
I see <u>my teachers</u> during the week, while I see <u>my grandparents</u> on the weekend.

**D**

Go to school
Do homework
Watch TV

See my friends
Study
Go to piano class

### Page 17

**F**

Sample response 1

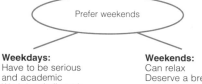

**Weekdays:**
Have to be serious
and academic
Work hard all week

**What you do:**
Go to school

**Weekends:**
Can relax
Deserve a break

**What you do:**
Can watch a movie
Do other things

**What you prefer:** Love weekends

Sample response 2

**Weekdays:**
Like to go to school
Student is job

**What you do:**
Like contributing thoughts
and ideas
See friends

**Weekends:**
Wastes time
Is dull

**What you do:**
Do nothing

**What you prefer:** Weekends great for some, not for me

**G**

1. serious
2. plus
3. academic
4. contribute
5. deserve

### Page 18

**Step 2**

Sample response 1

**Weekdays:**
Too busy
So much academic work

**What you do:**
Guitar lessons
Student Government

**Weekends:**
Some homework
Deserve a rest

**What you do:**
Go to church
Visit grandparents

**What you prefer:** Some people prefer weekdays, but I prefer weekends

Sample response 2

**Weekdays:**
More enjoyable

**What you do:**
See friends
Play computer games after school

**Weekends:**
Dull
Friends serious about schoolwork
Don't have time to meet

**What you do:**
Nothing interesting

**What you prefer:** Some people prefer weekdays, but I prefer weekdays

**Step 3**

Sample response 1

I prefer <u>weekends to weekdays</u>. I think that <u>weekdays are too busy</u> because <u>I have so much academic work. Plus, I take guitar lessons. I also contribute to our student government</u>. On <u>weekends, I do some homework but I deserve a rest, too. I also go to church and visit my grandparents</u>. Some people may prefer <u>weekdays</u>, but I much prefer <u>my weekends</u>.

Sample response 2
I prefer <u>weekdays to weekends</u>. I think that <u>my weekends are always so dull</u> because <u>my friends are too serious about their schoolwork</u>. <u>They do not take a break. And, they don't have time to meet me. So, I do nothing interesting. During the week is more enjoyable.</u> On <u>weekdays, I can see my friends and play computer games after school</u>. Some people may prefer <u>weekends</u>, but I much prefer <u>weekdays</u>.

## Integrated

### Page 19
**B**
1. The library will <u>stay open twenty-four hours a day, seven days a week</u>.
2. So that students can <u>prepare for their exams</u>.
3. I think the conversation will be about <u>how the change of hours will help the students</u>.

### Page 20
**B**

| Man | Woman |
|---|---|
| • Has an essay to <u>write for tomorrow</u><br>• It's fantastic because <u>he was having trouble getting work done</u><br>• Now has enough <u>time to study</u><br>• Can't study at home as it <u>is too noisy</u><br>• Does everything at <u>the library</u><br>• Now has <u>plenty time to finish his essay</u><br>• Will help <u>many people</u> | • First day of <u>new hours</u><br>• Final month of classes, so library open <u>24 hours a day</u><br>• Library is open <u>7 days a week</u><br>• Always studies at home, so <u>it won't make any difference</u> |

### Page 21
**D**
The man thinks the change in hours is <u>a great idea</u>.
A. It will give him more time
    1. to finish <u>essay</u>
    2. to study <u>for exams</u>
B. The man
    1. can't study <u>at home because of the noise</u>
    2. does everything <u>in the library</u>
C. He thinks the longer hours <u>will help many people</u>

**F**
1. permanent   2. due to   3. final
4. ordinary   5. access

### Page 22
**Step 2**

| Man | Woman |
|---|---|
| • Hears that the university is <u>changing hours at the computer lab</u><br>• Thinks it's <u>a great idea</u><br>• Has trouble accessing <u>a computer around final exams</u><br>• Thinks that would be best but <u>changing hours will help</u><br>• Thinks it's a <u>good point</u> | • Thinks changing hours won't <u>make a difference</u><br>• Need more <u>computers</u><br>• Works there, so will have to <u>get up early</u><br>• Doubts many students <u>will go at 7 a.m.</u><br>• Sounds permanent but they <u>will pay workers more</u><br>• Should use <u>that money to buy more computers</u><br>• Then many students could <u>use computers and not come in early</u> |

### Page 23
**Step 4**

The woman is <u>not happy about the change in the computer lab hours</u>.
A. The woman
    1. works at the <u>computer lab</u>
    2. will have to <u>get up earlier</u>
B. She thinks
    1. it will not help because <u>students won't use computers so early</u>
    2. the university should <u>use the money to buy more computers</u>

**Step 5**

The woman is <u>not happy about the change in the computer lab hours</u>. She works at the computer lab, so <u>she will have to get up earlier</u>. She thinks <u>it will not help</u> because most students <u>won't use the computers so early in the morning</u>. Therefore, instead of paying workers more, the university should <u>use the money to buy more computers</u>.

## Check-up

### Page 24
1. trouble   2. resume   3. exam
4. break   5. thoughts   6. Dull

# [ Unit 2 ]

**Independent**

**Page 25**

**B**

1. My best friend's name is <u>Kathy</u>.
2. I met my best friend <u>when my family moved to a new apartment two years ago</u>.
3. We like to <u>play computer games together</u>.

**Page 26**

**A**

1. I have an outgoing personality.
2. My friend has a shy personality.
3. Our personalities are very different.
4. I think this is good because we get to try new things with each other.

**B**

| | |
|---|---|
| Easy going | Adventurous |
| Quiet/shy | Talkative |
| Go with the flow | Outgoing |

**C**

One pastime that I enjoy doing with my friends is <u>playing soccer</u>.
We often go to <u>my house</u>.
Usually, we <u>play at least once a week after school</u>.
I like my friends because <u>we like to do the same things</u>.

**D**

| | |
|---|---|
| Playing computer games | Doing indoor activities |
| Listening to music | Watching movies |
| Reading | Playing sports |
| Doing outdoor activities | Chatting |

**Page 27**

**F**

Sample response 1

**My personality:**
Quiet

**My friend's personality:**
Adventurous

**Like to do:**
Indoor activities        Outdoor activities

**Best friends because:** Find each other interesting

Sample response 2

**My personality:**
Adventurous
Outgoing

**My friend's personality:**
Adventurous
Outgoing

**Like to do:**
Outdoor activities        Outdoor activities
Play soccer               Play soccer

**Best friends because:** Have fun together

**G**

1. personality    2. opposite    3. similar
4. activity       5. different

**Page 28**

**Step 2**

Sample response 1

**My personality:**
Talkative
Outgoing

**My friend's personality:**
Talkative
Outgoing

**Like to do:**
Chat                Chat
Outdoor activities  Outdoor activities

**Best friends because:** Lots to talk about

Sample response 2

**My personality:**
Easy going
Outgoing

**My friend's personality:**
Quiet
Shy

**Like to do:**
Watch movies        Watch movies
Go to parties

**Best friends because:** We do interesting things together

**Step 3**

Sample response 1

I think that best friends usually have <u>similar personalities</u>. A good example is me and my best friend. I am <u>talkative and outgoing</u> and my best friend is <u>also talkative and outgoing</u>. We like to <u>chat and do outdoor activities like rock climbing</u>. We are best friends because <u>we have lots to talk about</u>.

Sample response 2
I think that best friends usually have <u>opposite personalities</u>. A good example is me and my best friend. I am <u>easygoing and outgoing</u> and my best friend is <u>quiet and shy</u>. We like to <u>watch movies together and sometimes I take her to parties</u>. We are best friends because <u>we do interesting things when we are together</u>.

## Integrated

### Page 29
**B**
1. Impressionism was popular in <u>the 1800s</u> and it was started in <u>France</u>.
2. Impressionists painted <u>their experiences / nature and the outdoors / trees and lakes</u>.
3. I think the lecture will be about <u>Impressionist painters / how Impressionists painted / the Impressionists' style</u>.

### Page 30
**B**

Impressionists
- They painted things to <u>make them look real</u>
- Nineteenth century art supplies were <u>light</u>

Nature
- Artists painted <u>outdoors</u>
- Monet
  - painted in a <u>garden</u>
  - liked painting <u>outside</u>
  - did not have a real <u>studio</u>
- Nature often <u>changes</u>
- Speed was <u>important</u>

Colors
- Monet tried <u>different colors</u>
- Red, yellow, and green for <u>sunny paintings</u>
- Cloudy scenes used <u>gray and blue</u>

### Page 31
**D**

The lecture and passage were about <u>Monet and Impressionism</u>.
A. Impressionists liked to paint
  1. things in <u>nature</u>
  2. while <u>outside</u>
B. Monet
  1. liked to <u>paint outside</u>
  2. painted in <u>a garden</u>
  3. didn't have <u>a real studio</u>
C. Monet and other Impressionists
  1. painted <u>quickly</u>
  2. used different <u>colors to show how they saw the world</u>
Everything Monet did was <u>very normal for Impressionists</u>.

**F**
1. realistic    2. critics    3. influence
4. nature    5. medium

### Page 32
**Step 2**

Berthe Morisot
- She studied <u>drawing as a child</u>
- She began drawing and <u>painting outdoor scenes</u>
- Her parents were <u>happy</u>
- Her sisters were <u>her models</u>

Berthe Morisot's style
- It was <u>feminine</u>
- She used light <u>brush strokes</u>
- It was <u>realistic</u>

Berthe Morisot's paintings
- She painted <u>in nature</u>
- She liked to paint <u>trees, ponds, and lakes</u>
- She didn't like <u>crowds</u>

Berthe Morisot
- She died in <u>1895 at age 54</u>

### Page 33
**Step 4**

The passage and lecture were about <u>Berthe Morisot</u>.
A. Morisot
  1. was born <u>in 1841</u>
  2. started painting and drawing when <u>she was a child</u>
B. Her parents were <u>happy that she was an artist</u>.
C. Her sisters were <u>her models.</u>
D. Renoir and Degas influenced <u>her work</u>.
E. Morisot's style was <u>unique, feminine, and realistic</u>.
F. Morisot liked to paint people, <u>water, and trees</u>.

**Step 5**

The passage and lecture were about <u>Berthe Morisot</u>. She was born in <u>1841</u>. She started painting and drawing <u>as a child</u>. Her parents were <u>happy she was an artist. Her sisters were her models</u>. Also, artists like Renoir and Degas <u>influenced her</u>. Her style was <u>unique and feminine. Her painting was also realistic</u>. She liked to paint <u>people, water, and trees. She also liked to paint people resting or on boats</u>.

## Check-up

### Page 34
1. studio    2. outdoors    3. Speed
4. interesting    5. pastime    6. outgoing

# Answer Key

## [ Unit 3 ]

**Independent**

### Page 35

**B**

1. I use a <u>cell phone to make my phone calls</u>.
2. I use it <u>all the time</u>.
3. I <u>hate</u> to send text messages.

### Page 36

**A**

1. I send emails to my family and friends.
2. I have a blog. I use my blog to talk about what I do.
3. I look at my friends' photos.
4. I don't like using instant messaging because I don't like to type.

**B**

Music        Pictures
Videos       Journals
News        Schedules

**C**

I write letters <u>about once a year</u>.
I write letters to <u>my grandmother</u>.
I send letters because <u>she doesn't have email</u>.
I <u>hate</u> to send letters because <u>it takes such a long time</u>.

**D**

Email        Instant messaging
Telephone    Cell phone
Letter        Fax

### Page 37

**F**

Sample response 1

**First reason:**
Don't understand new technology
**Second reason:**
Telephones are very dependable
**Explain why:**
Computers complicated    Cell phones have bad reception
Telephones easy to use, available everywhere
**Think that:** Telephones are the best way to communicate

Sample response 2

**First reason:**
Anyone can use it
**Explain why:**
All friends use it
**Second reason:**
Have multiple conversations

Can send files
**Think that:** Love instant messaging

**G**

1. complicated    2. custom    3. Technology
4. dependable    5. multiple

### Page 38

**Step 2**

Sample response 1

**First reason:**
Custom of taking phone everywhere
**Second reason:**
Convenient
**Like because:**
Really fast at text messaging, best way to have a conversation
**Think that:** Love text messaging

Sample response 2

**First reason:**
Don't have to worry about reception
**Second reason:**
Dependable, multiple ways to log on
**Like because:** Friends use email, easier than text messaging
**Think that:** Email is best

**Step 3**

Sample response 1

I like to communicate by <u>text messaging</u>. It is great because <u>I now have the custom of taking my phone everywhere</u>. In addition, <u>it is really convenient</u>. I can <u>text really fast</u>. It is much easier <u>than emailing</u>. For me, <u>text messaging is the best way to have a conversation</u>.

Sample response 2

I like to communicate by <u>email</u>. It is great because <u>I don't have to worry about reception</u>. In addition, <u>it is dependable and there are multiple ways to log on</u>. I can <u>email my friends because they use email</u>. It is much easier <u>than text messaging</u>. For me, <u>emailing is the best way to keep in touch</u>.

## Integrated

### Page 39

**B**

1. The students are discussing if the woman should study in her hometown or move to another city.
2. The student says that it will be cheaper and that she can live with her parents.
3. I think the rest of the conversation will be about why she should move away.
4. I think the student should stay at home / move away.

### Page 40

**A**

| Reasons to stay home | Reasons to move away |
| --- | --- |
| • Cheaper because she could live at home<br>• Wouldn't have to fly home<br>• Knows the city very well<br>• Has a lot of friends<br>• See friends and family | • See a new city<br>• Meet new people<br>• Become more independent<br>• Have freedom<br>• Do new things |

**B**

1. The students discuss how living at home would be cheaper. Also she wouldn't have to fly home for the holidays and she knows the city well. In addition, she has a lot of friends in her hometown.
2. The student wants to move away because she could see a new city and meet new people. She could also be more independent and do what she wants.

### Page 41

**D**

The conversation is about whether the student should stay at home or move away for university.
A. Advantages of living at home
   1. It's cheaper because she could live with parents
   2. She knows the city well and has many friends
   3. She wouldn't have to fly home for the holidays
B. Advantages of living away
   1. See a new city and meet new people
   2. Become more independent, so have a more flexible lifestyle
Conclusion: I think she should stay at home as she will be more comfortable there and she won't miss her friends or family.

**E**

Conclusion: I think she should move away to a new city because university is a good time to become an adult and be free from your parents.

### G

1. decide    2. motivated    3. immediately
4. independent    5. flexible

### Page 42

**Step 1**

| Woman | Man |
| --- | --- |
| • Thinking of taking an online course<br>• Needs advice<br>• Will need to decide if it would be good for me | • The course is good<br>• Have to be motivated<br>• Make a schedule<br>• Also have to solve problems by yourself<br>• For an online course you have to email the professor<br>• It's flexible<br>• Have freedom<br>• It's cheaper<br>• An online degree is great for some people but not for others |

**Step 3**

The conversation is about online courses.
A. Student must
   1. be motivated
   2. make a schedule
   3. solve problems
B. Online you have to email the professor
C. Benefits
   1. It's flexible
   2. You have more freedom
   3. It's cheaper
Conclusion: I would prefer to study in a class because I need a teacher to help me and motivate me.

### Page 43

**Step 4**

The conversation is about online courses. The student must be motivated, make a schedule, and be able to solve problems alone. One problem with online courses is that you must email professors for help. Some advantages of online courses are that it's flexible, you have more freedom, and it's cheaper. I would prefer to study in a class because I need a teacher to help me and motivate me.

## Check-up

### Page 44

1. move away    2. cheap    3. Freedom
4. reception    5. old fashioned
6. conversations

# Answer Key

## [ Unit 4 ]

### Independent

**Page 45**

**B**

1. I live in a <u>big house</u>.
2. Near my house there are <u>a lot of parks and walking trails</u>.
3. The best thing about my home is <u>the beautiful view of the mountains from our backyard</u>.

**Page 46**

**A**

1. I can run around on the grass.
2. I like all the places to play outside.
3. The countryside has a lot less noise than the city.
4. Living in the countryside is good because it is much more relaxed than living in the city.

**B**

| | |
|---|---|
| Clean air | Big houses |
| Lots of space | Much quieter than the city |
| Laid back | Friendlier people |

**C**

Houses in the city are usually <u>small</u>.
In the city, there is a lot of <u>noise</u>.
At night, children must <u>be careful not to talk to strangers</u>.
Living in the city can be bad because <u>people are often in a rush</u>.

**D**

| | |
|---|---|
| Pollution | Hectic |
| Noisy | Exciting |
| Convenient | Fun |

**Page 47**

**F**

Sample response 1

**It is:**
More fun

**It is:**
Convenient

**It has:**
Sports games, museums, movie theaters
Shops close by

**Think that:** The city is better than the countryside

Sample response 2

**It is:**
Space

**It is:**
Healthy

**It has:**
Clean air
Space for kids to play

**Think that:** The countryside is a better place to live

**G**

1. disadvantage      2. include
3. advantages        4. convenient
5. moreover

**Page 48**

**Step 2**

Sample response 1

**It is:**
Convenient to shops, restaurants

**You can:**
Go to movie theaters

**It has:**
More to do

**Think that:** The city is better because there is so much to do

Sample response 2

Countryside is better

**It is:**
Healthier

**You can:**
Play in open space

**It has:**
Clean air

**Think that:** Countryside is better

**Step 3**

Sample response 1

I think that living in the <u>city</u> has more advantages than living in the <u>countryside</u>. The city has <u>more to do</u>. The countryside, unlike the city, has <u>fewer restaurants and no movie theaters</u>. <u>The city</u> is good because <u>there are so many restaurants</u>. Moreover, the <u>city has movie theaters</u>. Living in the <u>city</u> is better because <u>there is so much more to do</u>.

Sample response 2
I think that living in the <u>countryside</u> has more advantages than living in the <u>city</u>. The city has <u>a lot of pollution</u>. The countryside, unlike the city, has <u>clean air. The countryside</u> is good because <u>it is much healthier than the city</u>. Moreover, the <u>countryside has a lot of open space for kids to play</u>. Living in the <u>countryside</u> is better because <u>it is healthier</u>.

## Integrated

### Page 49

**B**

1. The lecture is about <u>Arctic animals</u>.
2. The most famous Arctic animal is <u>the polar bear</u>.
3. I think the professor will talk about <u>other Arctic animals</u>.

### Page 50

**A**

- Many Arctic animals
- They live on <u>land and in the sea</u>
- Land animals: <u>polar bears, caribou, and arctic hares</u>
- A caribou is <u>a kind of deer</u>
- A hare is <u>a kind of rabbit</u>
- Sea animals: <u>whales, seals, and walrus</u>
- The male narwhal has <u>a tusk</u>
- Sea <u>birds</u>
- Some migrate south <u>in winter</u>

**B**

1. The professor talks about <u>polar bears, caribou, and arctic hares</u>.
2. The professor gives <u>whales, seals, walrus, and birds</u> as examples of other Arctic animals.

### Page 51

**D**

The lecture is about <u>different Arctic animals</u>.
A. Land animals
  1. Polar bears: <u>most famous</u>
  2. Caribou: <u>like deer</u>
    - Its babies can <u>walk at a day old</u>
  3. Arctic hares: <u>like rabbits</u>
    - Lives in <u>herds</u>
B. Sea animals such as <u>whales, seals, and walrus</u>
C. Birds
  1. Some stay in <u>the Arctic all year</u>
  2. Some migrate <u>in winter</u>
Conclusion: Arctic animals <u>can adapt well to their environment.</u>

**F**

1. enemies    2. herds    3. adapt
4. migrate    5. dwelling

### Page 52

**Step 1**

- Polar animals are special
- They have to <u>adapt</u>
- Caribou and musk oxen eat <u>green plants</u>
- Foxes and wolves eat <u>other animals</u>
- The caribou migrate <u>south</u>
- Musk oxen have <u>long fur</u>
- Polar bears and whales have a <u>thick layer of fat</u>
- Some animals change <u>color</u>
- Arctic birds change from <u>brown</u> in summer to <u>white in winter</u>

**Step 3**

The lecture is about how polar animals live in the Arctic.
A. Food
  1. Caribou and musk oxen eat <u>plants</u>
  2. Foxes and wolves eat <u>other animals</u>
B. Protection from the cold
  1. Caribou <u>move south</u>
  2. Musk oxen have <u>long hair</u>
  3. Polar bears and whales have <u>thick fat</u>
C. Protection from enemies: <u>change color to hide</u>
Conclusion: Arctic animals have adapted well to their environment.

### Page 53

**Step 4**

The lecture is about <u>how polar animals live in the Arctic</u>. Arctic animals eat food that is easy to find. For example, <u>caribou eat plants and foxes eat other animals</u>. Arctic animals keep warm by <u>moving south and by having long fur or a thick layer of fat</u>. Arctic animals can hide because <u>they can change color in summer and winter</u>. They have adapted <u>well to their environment</u>.

## Check-up

### Page 54

1. tusks    2. Arctic    3. tundra
4. countryside  5. Unlike  6. air

# Answer Key

## [ Unit 5 ]

**Independent**

### Page 55

**B**
1. My favorite sport to play is <u>basketball</u>.
2. It is my favorite sport to play because <u>it is such a fast and competitive game</u>.
3. My favorite sport to watch is <u>American football</u>.

### Page 56

**A**
1. I usually go with my two brothers.
2. We usually climb trees and chase each other around.
3. We play in our backyard and at the park.
4. I feel great when I am finished playing outside.

**B**

| | |
|---|---|
| Tag | Chase |
| Soccer | Baseball |
| Talk | Race |

**C**
I like to <u>draw</u>.
I do this <u>by myself</u>.
I <u>draw a picture every day</u>.
I like to <u>draw</u> because <u>I am good at it</u>.

**D**

| | |
|---|---|
| Play computer games | Watch TV |
| Read books | Surf the Internet |
| Sleep | Cook |

### Page 57

**F**
Sample response 1

**First reason:**
Lets more friends participate

**Second reason:**
Feel energized

**Like because:**
More chances to socialize          Focus better on homework

**Think that:** Physical activities are much more fun

Sample response 2

**First reason:**
Love to read

**Second reason:**
Can read anywhere

**Like because:**
Connect with characters          Use your brain more

**Think that:** Nonphysical activities are much more fun

**G**
1. socializing   2. physical   3. connects
4. participate   5. nonphysical

### Page 58

**Step 2**
Sample response 1

**You can:**
Socialize

**You can:**
Get exercise

**Like because:**
Connect with people          Feel energized

**Think that:** Athletic sports are more fun

Sample response 2

Like nonphysical activities
(Chess)

**You can:**
Not get exhausted

**You can:**
Be social

**Like because:**
Can take it easy          Can exercise my mind

**Think that:** Nonphysical activities are relaxing and social

**Step 3**
Sample response 1
I prefer <u>to participate in physical activities, like basketball</u>. I like this because <u>I can socialize with my friends. I can connect with them while we play sports</u>. In addition, it allows me to <u>get exercise</u>. This is good because <u>it makes me feel energized</u>. I like <u>physical activities</u> because <u>athletic sports are fun and social</u>.

Sample response 2
I prefer <u>to participate in nonphysical activities, like chess</u>. I like this because <u>I don't get exhausted when I play. I can take it easy</u>. In addition, it allows me to <u>be social by playing with my friends</u>. This is good because <u>it allows me to connect with people and exercise my mind</u>. I like <u>nonphysical activities</u> because <u>they are relaxing and social</u>.

## Integrated

### Page 59

**B**

1. A new <u>study center will open</u>.
2. <u>Computer access and assistance from student tutors</u> will be available.
3. I think the conversation will be about <u>the new study center</u>.

### Page 60

**B**

| Man | Woman |
|---|---|
| • New study center will be <u>fantastic</u><br>• More access to <u>computers</u><br>• Get help with <u>homework from student tutors</u> | • Idea is <u>pointless</u><br>• Not enough <u>volunteers</u><br>• Students will have to <u>wait</u><br>• Only get <u>five minutes with helpers</u><br>• Helpers appointed <u>randomly</u><br>• Better to use money for <u>tutoring service</u> |

### Page 61

**D**

The conversation is about <u>the services offered at the new study center</u>.
A. The man says
   1. There will be <u>computers there</u>.
   2. There will be student <u>tutors to help with homework</u>.
B. The woman says
   1. There are not enough <u>student volunteers</u>.
   2. Students will <u>have to wait</u>.
   3. They will only have <u>five minutes with volunteers</u>.
C. She says that the university should <u>use money for a tutoring service</u>.

**F**

1. announced    2. available    3. randomly
4. appointed    5. frequent

### Page 62

**Step 2**

| Man | Woman |
|---|---|
| • No more <u>free tutors</u><br>• Wouldn't want them to <u>raise student fees</u><br>• Students too <u>busy to volunteer</u><br>• Advises woman to write to <u>the school paper</u> | • Thinks it's <u>awful</u><br>• Better to spend <u>less on sports</u><br>• Education should come <u>first</u><br>• Many students <u>need that free tutoring</u><br>• Professors will have <u>extra work</u> |

### Page 63

**Step 4**

The conversation is about <u>the announcement that the university will stop the free tutoring service</u>.
A. The woman's opinion of this is <u>that it is awful</u>
B. She says that the university should
   1. give less <u>money to sports</u>
   2. give more <u>money to educational services</u>
C. She thinks this because
   1. education should be <u>the most important thing</u>.
   2. a lot of students <u>need the free service</u>.

**Step 5**

The conversation is about <u>the announcement that the university will stop the free tutoring service</u>. The woman thinks that <u>stopping the free tutoring service is awful</u>. Instead, the university should <u>give less money to sports</u> and <u>give more money to educational services</u>. This is because she thinks <u>education is the most important thing at a university</u>. She adds that <u>a lot of students depend on the service</u>.

## Check-up

### Page 64

1. concerned    2. athletic    3. education
4. energizes    5. focus    6. pointless

# [ Unit 6 ]

## Independent

### Page 65

**B**

1. I usually buy <u>things to eat</u>.
2. I normally get money from <u>my part-time job</u>.
3. In the future, I want to buy <u>a car</u>.

### Page 66

**A**

1. The best thing that I bought was my fish tank.
2. I am happy that I spent money on my brother's birthday present.
3. I wish I hadn't spent money on playing video games because now I don't have anything to show for it.
4. I am excited about spending my money on some fish because I have a great home for them.

**B**

| | |
|---|---|
| Spend | Well-made |
| Great deal | Good value |
| Cheap | Expensive |

**C**

One time that I wasted money was when <u>I bought an expensive shirt</u>.

I bought this <u>six months ago</u>.

I bought this thing because <u>my friend said that the shirt looked really good on me</u>.

I wasted my money because <u>the shirt was ugly, and because it ripped two weeks later</u>.

**D**

| | |
|---|---|
| Useless | Rip off |
| Changed my mind | Too late to change |
| Too much | Too expensive |
| Can't afford it | |

## Page 67

**F**

Sample response 1

Spending money

**First reason:**
Like to have fun

**Second reason:**
Like to look fashionable

**What to do with it:**
Movies and concerts          New clothes

**This is good because:** Makes me feel happy

Sample response 2

Saving money

**First reason:**
Buy more expensive things

**Second reason:**
Have for emergency

**What to do with it:**
Buy computer          Can replace important things

**This is good because:** Makes me feel responsible

**G**

1. allow          2. modern          3. emergency
4. spare          5. fashion

## Page 68

**Step 2**

Sample response 1

Saving money

**First reason:**
Invest, make more money

**Second reason:**
Have money in an emergency

**Benefits:**
Don't work          Saved $100

**Why this is good:** Get more money

Sample response 2

Spending money

**First reason:**
Fun to buy things

**Second reason:**
Fun to do things

**Benefits:**
Get modern clothes          Play video games

**Why this is good:** Makes me happy

**Step 3**

Sample response 1

I think that it is better to <u>save</u> your money. I like to <u>invest</u> my money. It is good to have money for <u>emergencies</u>. Last year, I <u>saved one hundred dollars</u>. I also like to <u>make money without working by investing my money</u>. <u>Saving</u> my money is good because <u>it allows me to make more money</u>.

Sample response 2

I think that it is better to <u>spend</u> your money. I like to <u>buy things with</u> my money. It is good to have money for <u>modern, fashionable clothes</u>. Last year, I <u>bought a new jacket and some jeans</u>. I also like to <u>use my money to play video games</u>. <u>Spending</u> my money is good because <u>it makes me happy</u>.

### Integrated

## Page 69

**B**

1. Astronomy is the study of the <u>universe</u>.
2. Astronomers study the <u>planets and stars in our solar system</u>.
3. I think the lecture will be about <u>astronomy and our solar system</u>.

## Page 70

**B**

Astronomy
- Astronomers look at <u>the size and movement of planets</u>.
- They use <u>telescopes to see planets</u>.

Telescopes
- They are used because <u>planets are very far away</u>.
- Light takes <u>8 minutes to reach Earth from the Sun</u>.
- Sun is bright because <u>it is the closest star to us</u>.

How many planets now?
- There are <u>eight planets</u>.

## Page 71

**D**

The lecture and passage were about astronomy and the solar system.

A. Astronomers study
   1. the <u>universe</u>
   2. the size of planets and <u>their movement around the Sun</u>
B. Planets
   1. There used to be nine, now <u>only eight</u>
   2. We use telescopes because <u>the planets are far away</u>
C. The planets are <u>spheres like the Earth.</u>

**F**

1. consider   2. spheres   3. altogether
4. universe   5. explosions

## Page 72

**Step 2**

The moon
- orbits <u>the Earth</u>
- takes <u>one month to go around it</u>
- is the <u>only object in space people have visited</u>

You can
- see it with <u>your eyes, binoculars or a telescope</u>
- see a full <u>moon once a month</u>
- use a telescope to <u>see craters on the moon</u>

When
- it is bright we see <u>sunlight reflected off it</u>
- it goes between us and the Sun <u>it is called an eclipse</u>
- we always see <u>the same side of the moon</u>

## Page 73

**Step 4**

The passage and lecture were about
A. The moon
   1. orbits <u>the Earth</u>
   2. takes <u>one month to go around the Earth</u>
   3. is the only object <u>in space that people have visited</u>
B. You can
   1. see it <u>with your eyes, binoculars, or a telescope</u>
   2. see a full moon <u>once a month</u>
   3. use a telescope <u>to see craters on it</u>
   4. always see same <u>side</u>
C. It is covered in <u>big holes called craters</u>

**Step 5**

The passage and lecture were about <u>the moon</u>. It orbits the <u>Earth</u>. It takes <u>one month</u> to do this. And you only see a <u>full moon</u> one a month. You can see it clearly with your <u>eyes, binoculars, or with a telescope</u>. When you do see it, you always see <u>the same side</u>. It is <u>covered in big holes called craters</u>.

## Page 74

1. save        2. telescopes   3. craters
4. spend       5. astronomers  6. concerts

# [ Review 1 ]

**Independent 1**

## Page 75

**Step 2**

Sample response 1

**Studying on your own**        **Studying with friends**
Benefits:
Can concentrate

Drawbacks:
Can't discuss your thoughts    Many distractions
**Better because:** Can do more work


Sample response 2

**Studying on your own**        **Studying with friends**
Benefits:

                               Help each other
                               Discuss

Drawbacks:
Can't talk about your work     Distractions
**Better because:** It makes studying more interesting


**Step 3**

Sample response 1
When I study, I prefer to do it <u>on my own</u>. I like it because <u>I can concentrate on my work</u>. It can have disadvantages, though; you <u>can't discuss your thoughts because there is no one to talk to</u>. I prefer not to study <u>with friends</u> because <u>there are too many distractions</u>. Studying <u>on my own</u> is better because <u>I can get more work done</u>.


Sample response 2
When I study, I prefer to do it <u>with friends</u>. I like it because <u>we can talk about what we are doing and help each other</u>. It can have disadvantages, though; you <u>can get distracted easily</u>. I prefer not to study on my own because I <u>cannot talk about my work with anyone</u>. Studying <u>with friends</u> is better because <u>it makes it more interesting</u>.

# Answer Key

## Integrated 1

Page 76

**Step 2**

| Man | Woman |
|-----|-------|
| • The announcement is <u>a stupid idea</u> | • Did not <u>go to the cafeteria for lunch</u> |
| • For lunch, he goes <u>to the cafeteria every day</u> | • Goes to <u>the shops for her lunch</u> |
| • At the cafeteria, he <u>sits and studies while he eats his lunch</u> | • Suggests that the man could <u>leave the school for his lunch</u> |
| • Thinks the school should stop <u>the students from leaving at lunch time</u> | • She thinks that the school <u>will not change their mind</u> |
| • He wants to <u>speak to other students and the school about it</u> | |

Page 77

**Step 4**

The conversation is about <u>the school's decision to close down the cafeteria</u>.
A. The man's opinion of this is it is a <u>terrible idea</u>
B. He says that this is because
  1. he uses the <u>cafeteria every day</u>
  2. he likes to <u>study there</u>
C. He says that he should
  1. talk to some <u>of the other students</u>
  2. speak to the school and <u>get them to change their minds</u>

**Step 5**

He thinks closing the school cafeteria is <u>a terrible idea</u>. This is because <u>he uses the cafeteria every day</u>. In addition to eating there, <u>he likes to study there</u>. He says that <u>he's going to talk to some other students</u>. He also wants to <u>speak to the school to see if he can get them to change their minds</u>.

## Integrated 2

Page 78

**Step 1**

- A business is a company
- It sells <u>goods and services to people</u>
- They can be very <u>small or very big</u>
- Most start <u>off small and become big with profit</u>
- When Google started, its office <u>was in a garage</u>
- Over time, and when its <u>technology got better and adapted</u>, it became more popular
- Now it is known <u>all over the world</u>
- A company is better when its <u>goods or services are more convenient</u>

**Step 3**

The lecture is about businesses and improving them over time.
A. In the beginning
  1. companies are <u>small</u>
  2. do not make much <u>profit</u>
B. Over time
  1. they become <u>more successful</u>
  2. goods or services <u>get better and more convenient</u>
C. Google is a company that
  1. began <u>in a garage</u>
  2. is now known and used <u>all over the world</u>
Conclusion: Businesses take time to improve and get better.

Page 79

**Step 4**

The lecture is about <u>businesses and improving them over time</u>. In the beginning, businesses <u>are small and don't make much profit</u>. However, over time <u>they become more successful. Their goods and services also get better and more convenient</u>. Google is a an example of a <u>company that began in a garage and is now known and used by people all over the world</u>. Businesses take time to <u>improve and get better</u>.

## Independent 2

Page 80

**Step 2**
Sample response 1

Teachers should be fun

**Fun teachers**          **Strict teachers**
Good points:
Keep me interested

Bad points:                  Boring
                             No fun

**I prefer:** Fun teachers because they are entertaining

Sample response 2

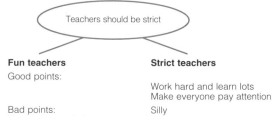

Teachers should be strict

**Fun teachers**          **Strict teachers**
Good points:

                           Work hard and learn lots
                           Make everyone pay attention
Bad points:                  Silly
Hard to concentrate

**I prefer:** Strict teachers because I learn more

## Step 3
Sample response 1
When I am in class, I like to <u>have fun when I am learning</u>. I like <u>fun</u> teachers because <u>they keep me interested in class</u>. I don't like <u>strict</u> teachers because <u>they can be boring and stop me from having fun</u>. My favorite kind of teacher is <u>a fun teacher</u> because <u>they can teach and entertain at the same time</u>.

Sample response 2
When I am in class, I like to <u>work hard and learn as much as I can</u>. I like <u>strict</u> teachers because <u>they make everyone pay attention</u>. I don't like <u>fun</u> teachers because <u>they are silly and it is hard to concentrate</u>. My favorite kind of teacher is <u>a strict teacher</u> because <u>they make sure I learn as much as I can</u>.

# [ Unit 7 ]

## Independent

### Page 81
B
1. My favorite subject is <u>history</u> because <u>I find history to be so interesting</u>.
2. My least favorite subject is <u>English</u> because <u>I do not really like writing</u>.

### Page 82
A
1. Yes, I like my science class.
2. I do experiments with electricity.
3. I usually do very well in this class.
4. I learn about how our bodies work.

B

| | |
|---|---|
| Dissection | Mixtures |
| Results | Electricity |
| How things work | How to make things |
| Experiment | |

C
I prefer going to <u>art class</u>.
My favorite kind of art to make is <u>sculpture</u>.
I practice music <u>three times a week</u>.
I play <u>the piano</u>.

D

| | |
|---|---|
| Sculpting | Drawing |
| Feelings | Recorder |
| Guitar | Inspirational |
| Creativity | |

### Page 83
F
Sample response 1

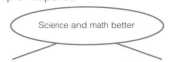

**First reason:** See results
**Second reason:** Achieve goals
**Like because:** Tells right away if you are correct or not
**I prefer:** Science

Sample response 2

**First reason:** Express feelings
**Second reason:** Inspirational
**Like because:** I am good at them and it feels good
**I prefer:** Humanities because everyone can do it

G
1. inspirational   2. achieve   3. humanities
4. particular   5. express

### Page 84
Step 2
Sample response 1

**First reason:** Expresses feelings
**Second reason:** Be creative
**Like because:** Help me understand myself
Don't have to study hard
**I prefer:** Drawing and painting because I am good at them

Sample response 2

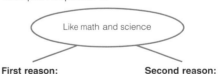

**First reason:** Both challenging
**Second reason:** Feel inspired
**Like because:** Science class gives sense of achievement
**I prefer:** Math and science because they are interesting but difficult

Step 3
Sample response 1
I like <u>art and music best</u>. I think these subjects <u>allow me to express my feelings</u>. I think they help me <u>understand myself</u>. I especially like <u>painting and drawing</u>. I like to <u>be creative</u>, so this class is good for me. I usually <u>don't have</u> to study hard for these subjects because <u>I am good at them</u>.

# Answer Key

Sample response 2
I like <u>math and science</u>. I think these subjects <u>are both challenging</u>. I think they help me <u>feel inspired</u>. I especially like <u>science class</u>. I like to <u>feel a sense of achievement</u>, so this class is good for me. I usually <u>have</u> to study hard for these subjects because <u>they are interesting but difficult</u>.

## Integrated

### Page 85

**B**

1. The students are discussing <u>if the male student should go abroad for summer vacation or stay home</u>.
2. The student says <u>that it would be a lot of fun and he would experience a new culture</u>.
3. I think the rest of the conversation will be about <u>what the student could do at home.</u>
4. I think the student should <u>go to France and experience French culture</u>.

### Page 86

**A**

| Man | Woman |
|---|---|
| • Two choices: <u>visit France or visit grandparents</u><br>• Traveling might <u>difficult</u><br>• Doesn't <u>speak French</u><br>• Doesn't have <u>a lot of time</u><br>• Would miss <u>his friends</u><br>• Staying might be <u>boring</u><br>• Won't meet <u>new people</u><br>• Could <u>save money</u> | • Working with <u>her dad</u><br>• Thinks traveling might be <u>fun</u><br>• He could experience <u>a new culture</u><br>• Thinks the man could learn <u>French</u><br>• Might be nice to <u>stay here</u><br>• Could spend time <u>relaxing</u><br>• Thinks man's summer will be <u>better than hers</u> |

**B**

1. The students discuss <u>traveling abroad because it would be fun and interesting. Also, he could learn French. Staying home might be boring</u>.
2. The students discuss <u>staying home because it would be relaxing, and the student would miss his friends if he traveled. Also, it would be difficult to go to France because he doesn't speak French</u>.

### Page 87

**D**

The conversation is about <u>the students' summer vacation plans</u>.
A. Advantages of traveling abroad
  1. Experience <u>a new culture</u>
  2. Visit <u>some museums</u>

B. Disadvantages of traveling abroad
  1. Miss <u>his friends</u>
  2. Can't speak <u>French</u>
C. Advantages of staying home
  1. <u>Relaxing</u>
  2. <u>Save money</u>
D. Disadvantages of staying home
  1. <u>Boring</u>
  2. Wouldn't meet <u>new people</u>
Conclusion: I think <u>he should travel to France because it is more interesting</u>.

**E**

Conclusion: I think he should <u>stay home for his summer vacation</u> because <u>he can save money and it's important to spend time with your family and friends</u>.

**G**

1. youth    2. responsibility    3. interests
4. culture    5. relax

### Page 88

**Step 1**

| Man | Woman |
|---|---|
| • Found a job?<br>• I will work at a <u>summer camp</u><br>• I like having <u>extra money</u><br>• I'm saving for <u>tuition</u><br>• I'm going to buy a <u>new cell phone</u><br>• I have met <u>some great people</u><br>• We have same <u>interests</u><br>• Hurry if you want to find a good job | • No, I'm not sure<br>• I like having <u>freedom</u><br>• I can <u>stay up late</u><br>• Not <u>worry about work</u><br>• Having a job is a lot of <u>responsibility</u><br>• I want to <u>earn money</u><br>• I want to enjoy my <u>youth</u> |

**Step 3**

The conversation is about <u>having a summer job or not.</u>
A. Advantages of having a summer job
  1. Can earn <u>money</u>
    • can buy <u>cell phone</u>
  2. Can make new <u>friends</u>
    • have same <u>interests</u>
B. Disadvantages of having a summer job
  1. No <u>freedom</u>
    • have to think about <u>work</u>
  2. A lot of <u>responsibility</u>
C. Can't decide
  1. Want to <u>earn money</u>
  2. Also want to <u>enjoy youth</u>
Conclusion: I would prefer <u>not to have a summer job and have my freedom</u>.

## Page 89

### Step 4

The conversation is about <u>having a summer job or not</u>. The male student already has a job at a summer camp. He likes having a summer job because he can <u>earn money</u> and then he can <u>buy things</u>. Also, he can meet <u>new friends</u> who have <u>the same interests</u>. The female student likes her <u>freedom and</u> she doesn't have to <u>think about her job</u>. Also, having a job is a lot of <u>responsibility</u>. She wants to <u>earn money</u> but she also wants to <u>enjoy her youth</u>. I would prefer <u>not to have a summer job and have my freedom</u>.

### Check-up

### Page 90

1. subjects
2. vacation
3. feelings
4. correct
5. decision
6. definitely

# [ Unit 8 ]

### Independent

### Page 91

**B**

1. I like to watch <u>comedies</u>.
2. I usually watch TV for <u>an hour and a half every day</u>.
3. I watch TV <u>for half an hour in the morning, and an hour at night</u>.

### Page 92

**A**

1. My favorite TV show is *The Simpsons*.
2. My favorite person on the show is Homer Simpson.
3. I like the show because it is so clever and funny at the same time.
4. The show is really popular because everyone can find something funny in it.

**B**

| | |
|---|---|
| Entertaining | Dramatic |
| Hilarious | Exciting |
| Clever and smart | Artistic and daring |
| Great influence | |

**C**

The TV show that affected me was <u>the evening news</u>. I always watch this TV show <u>at home with my parents</u>. After watching the show, I <u>would talk about what happened with my mom</u>.
The TV show has changed me because <u>I learned that it is important to know what is happening around me</u>.

**D**

| | |
|---|---|
| Bad influence | Bad habit |
| Violence | Lazy |
| Idiot box | Unhealthy |

### Page 93

**F**

Sample response 1

**First reason:**
Connect children with much content

**Second reason:**
Positive messages to kids

**Think this because:**
See things they don't usually    Help kids grow up

**Think that:** TV helps children in many ways.

Sample response 2

**First reason:**
Too violent

**Second reason:**
Unhealthy

**Think this because:**
Kids copy behavior    Don't go outside to play

**Think that:** It shows kids bad habits.

**G**

1. positive
2. In addition
3. content
4. reduce
5. messages

### Page 94

### Step 2

Sample response 1

**First reason:**
Content is educational

**Second reason:**
Can teach children about the world

**Think this because:**
Children know more about other countries
Helps kids understand other cultures

**Think that:** TV is great for kids

Sample response 2

TV has a negative influence on children

**First reason:**
Too many cartoons

**Second reason:**
Wastes time

**Think this because:**
Spend too much time indoors    TV leads to problems in school

**Think that:** TV is bad for kids

# Answer Key

## Step 3

**Sample response 1**

I think television has a <u>positive</u> influence on children. One reason I think this is because <u>much of the content on television is educational</u>. Television can <u>teach children about the world</u>. Children who watch a lot of television <u>know more about other countries</u>. Watching a lot of TV can <u>help kids understand other cultures</u>. TV is <u>great for kids</u> because <u>it exposes them to so many different ideas</u>.

**Sample response 2**

I think television has a <u>negative</u> influence on children. One reason I think this is because <u>there are too many cartoons on TV</u>. Television can <u>waste a lot of time</u>. Children who watch a lot of television <u>spend too much time indoors</u>. Watching a lot of TV can <u>lead to problems in school</u>. TV is <u>bad for kids</u> because <u>it wastes time when they could be learning</u>.

## Integrated

### Page 95

**B**

1. The lecture is about <u>acid rain</u>.
2. Acid rain is formed when <u>coal, oil, or wood are burned</u>.
3. I think the professor will talk about <u>ways to reduce acid rain</u>.

### Page 96

**A**

- Acid rain contains sulfur and <u>nitrogen</u>.
- It forms when coal, oil, or <u>wood are burned</u>.
- We burn coal to make <u>electricity</u>.
- We use electricity in <u>homes and factories</u>.
- We burn oil to make cars go and to <u>make airplanes fly</u>.
- This releases sulfur and nitrogen <u>gases that float into the sky</u>.
- The gases mix with <u>water drops in clouds</u>.
- It is bad for plants and <u>animals</u>.
- It makes acid rain that is <u>dangerous</u>.
- It is a big <u>problem</u>.

**B**

1. The professor gives the example of <u>burning coal to make electricity</u>.
2. The professor explains that gases float <u>up into the sky, into the clouds</u>, and mix with <u>water drops</u> to form <u>acid rain</u>.

### Page 97

**D**

The lecture is about <u>acid rain</u>.
A. Acid rain forms when we burn
  1. coal
  2. oil
  3. wood
B. We burn these things to
  1. make electricity for <u>homes and factories</u>
  2. make <u>cars go</u>
  3. make <u>airplanes fly</u>
C. This releases
  1. <u>sulfur</u>
  2. <u>nitrogen gases</u>
D. The gases float <u>up into clouds</u> and mix with <u>water drops</u>.
Conclusion: Acid rain kills <u>plants and animals</u> and is <u>dangerous and a big problem</u>.

**F**

1. damage   2. forms   3. released
4. contains   5. structure

### Page 98

**Step 1**

- Acid rain does a lot of <u>harm.</u>
- It damages buildings made of sandstone and <u>limestone</u>.
- It makes holes in them and damages their <u>structure</u>.
- Acid rain hurts plants and animals that <u>live in water</u>.
- Acid burns them and kills the <u>insects they feed on</u>.
- It kills fish and fish <u>eggs</u>.
- Birds <u>can get sick</u>.
- Acid rain damages leaves and <u>runs into the soil</u>.
- Then plants can't grow because the soil is <u>too acid</u>.

**Step 3**

The lecture is about how acid rain does a lot of harm.
A. Damage to buildings made of <u>sandstone and limestone</u>
  1. by making <u>holes in them</u>
  2. by damaging their <u>structure</u>
B. Burns or kills water plants and animals
  1. Kills insects <u>they feed on</u>
  2. Kills <u>fish and fish eggs</u>
  3. Makes <u>birds sick</u>
C. Damages forests
  1. Damages <u>leaves</u>
  2. Makes soil too acidic for <u>plants to grow</u>
Conclusion: Acid rain must be stopped.

**Page 99**

**Step 4**

Acid rain does <u>a lot of harm</u>. It can damage <u>buildings made of sandstone and limestone by making holes in them. This damages their structure</u>. It burns or kills water <u>plants and animals</u>. Acid rain kills insects <u>that are food for water animals</u>. It kills fish and <u>fish eggs</u>. <u>It makes birds sick too</u>. It damages forests <u>and the leaves of trees and makes soil too acidic for plants to grow</u>. Acid rain <u>must be stopped</u>.

## Check-up

**Page 100**

1. acid     2. violent     3. habit
4. behavior     5. float     6. mix

# [ Unit 9 ]

## Independent

**Page 101**

**B**

1. I need <u>to be in a quiet environment</u>.
2. I like to <u>drink coffee</u> while studying.
3. I prefer to study <u>late at night</u>.

**Page 102**

**A**

1. I finish school every day at 3 o'clock.
2. The first thing that I do when I come home is take a nap.
3. Yes, I do. I go to tae kwon do school.
4. I exercise every day by playing soccer.

**B**

| | |
|---|---|
| Check email | Playing with friends |
| Play on the play ground | Get a snack |
| Go swimming | Do homework |

**C**

I usually have homework for <u>math, science, history and English</u>.
I usually do my homework <u>in my dad's office</u>.
I typically have <u>2</u> hours of homework every day.
My <u>science</u> teacher gives me the most homework.

**D**

| | |
|---|---|
| Teacher | Homework |
| Routine | Discipline |
| Challenge | Science |
| Math | Social studies |

**Page 103**

**F**

Sample response 1

**First reason:**     **Second reason:**
Because rather be playing     It isn't useful
**Don't like because:**
I get good grades without homework
**Think that:** Comprehend the first time, so should spend more time on work.

Sample response 2

**First reason:**     **Second reason:**
Need repetition and routine     teaches discipline
**Like because:**
Is vital to my success     Will need this later
**Think that:** I enjoy the challenge, so I'm happy to do it.

**G**

1. manage     2. discipline     3. vital
4. challenge     5. routine

**Page 104**

**Step 2**

Sample response 1

**First reason:**     **Second reason:**
Think about lessons     Forces to remember
**Do/don't like because:**
Would rather be out with friends
Homework is good for me
Often interesting
**Think that:** Homework is important

Sample response 2

**First reason:**     **Second reason:**
Boring     Miss activities
    Prevents me from watching TV
**Do/don't like because:**
Rather be out with friends
Parents make me do it
**Think that:** Homework is the worst part of the day

# Answer Key

## Step 3
### Sample response 1
I <u>like doing</u> homework. I think homework is <u>a great way for me to learn</u>. Homework makes me <u>think about the lessons I heard in school and forces me to remember them</u>. I would rather <u>be out playing with my friends, but I know doing my homework is good for me</u>. In addition, homework <u>is often interesting</u>. Homework is <u>important</u> because <u>it helps me to learn</u>.

### Sample response 2
I <u>hate to do my</u> homework. I think homework is <u>boring</u>. Homework makes me <u>miss a lot of fun activities like playing with my friends</u>. I would rather <u>be out playing with my friends, but my parents make me do my homework</u>. In addition, homework <u>prevents me from watching TV</u>. Homework is <u>the worst part of my day</u> because <u>it keeps me from doing the things I enjoy</u>.

## Integrated

### Page 105
**B**
1. The Health Sciences Department will <u>increase professors' office hours</u>.
2. Students should <u>ask their professors to tell them their new hours</u>.
3. I think the conversation will be about <u>the announcement to change professors' office hours</u>.

### Page 106
**B**

| Man | Woman |
|---|---|
| • Professors are <u>increasing office hours</u> | • Wants to know if change will affect <u>whole campus</u> |
| • It is only for the <u>Health Sciences Department</u> | • Change doesn't help her because she is a <u>business major</u> |
| • Thinks announcement is <u>great</u> | |
| • Professor's hours conflict <u>with schedule</u> | |
| • Always has classes <u>during them</u> | |
| • Lots of students are having <u>the same problem</u> | |
| • Has to <u>ask professors for their new hours after class</u>. | |
| • Needs <u>help with a few classes</u> | |

### Page 107
**D**
The conversation is about <u>the increase in office hours for professors in the Health Sciences Department</u>.
A. The man thinks <u>the decision is great</u>.
B. He thinks this because
1. he can't see his professors during <u>office hours because he always has class</u>.
2. many other students have <u>the same problem he does</u>.
C. He needs to get help with <u>some of his classes during the new office hours</u>.
Conclusion: He is very <u>happy with the announcement</u>.

**F**
1. demand    2. respond    3. conflicts
4. dedicated    5. advance

### Page 108
**Step 2**

| Man | Woman |
|---|---|
| • Wants to form a <u>study group in his sociology class</u> | • Thinks it's a great idea, so wants to discuss <u>class work</u> |
| • Wonders where they can <u>meet</u> | • Suggest the <u>library</u> because <u>they have dedicated rooms to group study</u> |
| • Thinks the news is <u>wonderful</u> | • Can't go to <u>quiet places for discussions</u> |
| • His literature group meets in the <u>cafeteria</u> | • Might <u>bother others</u> |
| • Problem there is it gets <u>noisy</u> | |
| • Suggests they <u>reserve a room before class</u> | |

### Page 109
**Step 4**

The conversation is about <u>the library's plan to dedicate rooms to group study</u>.
A. The man's opinion of this is <u>it's wonderful</u>.
B. He thinks this because his study group <u>usually meets in the cafeteria but it is too noisy</u>.
C. You can't have discussions <u>in quiet places because you might bother others</u>.

**Step 5**
He thinks dedicating rooms in the library to study groups is <u>a wonderful idea</u>. Right now his study group <u>meets at the cafeteria</u>. But he doesn't like it because <u>it gets too noisy</u>. That's why he <u>likes the idea</u>. The woman adds that you can't <u>do group study in quiet places</u>. This is because you might <u>bother others</u>.

## Check-up

### Page 110
1. timetable    2. rather    3. comprehend
4. success    5. unexpected    6. inform

# [ Unit 10 ]

**Independent**

**Page 111**

**B**

1. I <u>like</u> gym class because <u>I can run around with my friends</u>.
2. My favorite part of gym class is <u>when we play dodge ball</u>.
3. My least favorite part of gym class is <u>when the teacher tells us to go back to class</u>.

**Page 112**

**A**

1. I like to go skiing for my exercise.
2. I try to exercise four times a week.
3. I feel tired but really healthy after I exercise.
4. Exercise helps me sit down and focus because I can run around and get my energy out.

**B**

| | |
|---|---|
| Healthy | Jogging |
| Walking | Strong, healthy |
| Exhausted | Sore |

**C**

Children should exercise <u>during their free time at school</u>.
Children should exercise <u>every day</u>.
Children should <u>run around</u> when they exercise.
They should exercise because <u>it makes them strong and healthy</u>.

**D**

| | |
|---|---|
| Soccer | Basketball |
| Tennis | Football |
| Swimming | |

**Page 113**

**F**

Sample response 1

**First reason:**
Maintain healthy lifestyle
**Second reason:**
Overweight children
**Should do this:**
Make kids exercise
Teach important habits
**Think that:** P.E. helps kids now as well as in the future.

Sample response 2

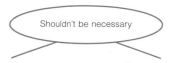

**First reason:**
Children falling behind
**Second reason:**
Many places to play after school
**Should do this:**
Make it optional
Spend more time studying.
**Think that:** P.E. is important but it shouldn't be in school.

**G**

1. maintained    2. necessity    3. balance
4. optional      5. suggest

**Page 114**

**Step 2**
Sample response 1

**First reason:**
Makes sure children exercise
**Second reason:**
Teaches kids the necessity of a healthy lifestyle
**Do this:**
Exercise to be healthy
**Conclusion:**
P.E. is necessary

Sample response 2

**First reason:**
P.E. wastes time
**Second reason:**
Exercise doesn't need to be part of school
**Do this:**
Children should exercise after school
**Conclusion:** P.E. isn't necessary

**Step 3**
Sample response 1
I think that <u>Physical Education should be required in all schools</u>. Physical Education is <u>the best way to make sure children get enough exercise.</u> Exercise is important because <u>it helps us remain healthy.</u> P.E. <u>teaches kids the necessity of a healthy lifestyle</u>. P.E. doesn't <u>take time from studying</u>. P.E. is necessary because <u>we must have exercise to maintain a healthy lifestyle</u>.

# Answer Key

Sample response 2
I think that <u>Physical Education should be an optional class in our schools</u>. Physical Education is <u>a waste of time that prevents students from studying</u>. Exercise is important because <u>it helps us have balance in our lives, but I suggest that children should increase the amount of exercise they get after school</u>. P.E. doesn't <u>need to be part of the school day</u>. P.E. isn't necessary because <u>children can exercise after school</u>.

## Integrated

**Page 115**

**B**
1. People can watch <u>television</u> and listen to <u>the radio</u>.
2. People used to <u>read, tell stories, play music, or go to the theater</u>.
3. I think the lecture will be about <u>technology and entertainment</u>.

**Page 116**

**B**

Technology
- The effect on our lives <u>is huge</u>
- Before it, people were <u>limited</u>
- Now we have <u>many choices</u>

Examples
- We can use the <u>TV, radio, and computer</u>
- We use them for <u>having fun</u>
- Outside we can <u>play with our phones and listen to music</u>
- We can even watch <u>TV on our phones now</u>

Technology
- Progress <u>is very quick now</u>
- It is easy to have fun <u>in our homes now</u>
- We do not have to <u>go out</u>

**Page 117**

**D**

The lecture and passage were about <u>technology in entertainment</u>
A. It has a huge effect on <u>the way we relax</u>
B. In the past
   1. people used to <u>read books, tell stories, or go to the theater</u>
   2. they did this <u>for fun</u>
C. Nowadays
   1. we also <u>watch TV, listen to the radio, and play on the computer</u>
   2. we can even do this <u>outside</u>
D. Things are changing <u>quickly</u>
E. Because of technology, we can do <u>more things more easily</u>

**F**
1. entertainment  2. gradually  3. progress
4. channel     5. Currently

**Page 118**

**Step 2**

Television
- lets us see <u>moving pictures</u>
- lets us hear <u>sounds</u>

To begin with
- there were only <u>a few channels</u>
- they were <u>small</u>
- pictures were in <u>black and white</u>

As technology moves on
- we can watch and record <u>hundreds of channels</u>
- you can choose what each one <u>will show</u>
- people can buy <u>movies and programs on disc</u>
- you can play <u>music, DVDs, and video games with TV</u>

In the future
- you will be able to <u>do even more</u>

**Page 119**

**Step 4**

The passage and lecture were about <u>television and entertainment</u>
A. Television became popular <u>in the late 1930s</u>
   1. The pictures were <u>in black and white</u>
   2. It lets us see <u>moving pictures and hear sounds</u>
B. With TV today
   1. You can watch <u>hundreds of channels</u>
   2. You can play <u>music, DVDs, and video games</u>
C. In the future
   1. You will be able to do <u>even more with your TV</u>
   2. You will have <u>more choice</u>

**Step 5**

The passage and lecture were about <u>television in entertainment</u>. Television became popular <u>in the late 1930s</u>. To begin with, the pictures were <u>in black and white</u>. Television lets us see <u>moving pictures</u> and hear <u>sounds</u>. With TV today you can watch and record <u>hundreds of channels</u>. On a TV, you can play <u>music, DVDs, and video games</u>. In the future you will be able to do <u>even more with your TV</u>. You will have even <u>more choice</u>.

## Check-up

**Page 120**

1. remote control  2. lifestyle  3. waste
4. huge        5. increase  6. theater

# [ Unit 11 ]

**Independent**

## Page 121

**B**

1. I dislike <u>how slow it is</u>.
2. An advantage of traveling by sea is <u>that it is usually cheaper</u>.
3. An advantage of traveling by land is <u>you can stop when you need to</u>.

## Page 122

**A**

1. Yes, I have been on an airplane.
2. I usually watch the movie on the flight.
3. I feel really tired after flying.
4. I don't like flying on an airplane because it's too crowded.

**B**

| | |
|---|---|
| Read magazines | Sleep |
| Jet lagged | Stiff |
| Sore | No space |
| Crying babies | Hectic |

**C**

I <u>sat on the beach.</u>
I went to <u>Thailand</u>.
I got there by <u>airplane</u>.
I went with <u>my friend</u>.

**D**

| | |
|---|---|
| Hiking | Swimming |
| Visit friend's family | Sightseeing |
| Scuba diving | Beach |

## Page 123

**F**

Sample response 1

**First reason:**
Gives freedom

**Second reason:**
Hate going to the airport

**Like because:**
Independent person

**Think that:** Will always drive in car

Sample response 2

**First reason:**
No effort

**Second reason:**
Don't have to worry about anything

**Like because:**
Fall asleep and arrive
Wake up in a new city

**Think that:** Fast and easy, so loves flying

**G**

1. effort    2. located    3. mode
4. supposed to 5. require

## Page 124

**Step 2**

Sample response 1

**First reason:**
Fast

**Second reason:**
Less hectic

**Like because:**
Arrive sooner
Enjoy view from the sky

**Think that:** Airplane is the best way to fly

Sample response 2

**First reason:**
Inexpensive

**Second reason:**
Easier

**Like because:**
Requires less effort
Like the scenery

**Think that:** Train or boat is the best way to travel

**Step 3**

Sample response 1
I prefer to travel by <u>airplane</u>. I like traveling by <u>airplane</u> because <u>it is the fastest mode of transportation, so I get to my destination sooner. It is best because I don't have to worry about being late so it seems less hectic.</u> I like to travel by <u>airplane</u> because <u>I get bored on a boat or a train</u>. In addition, I like <u>to see the cities from the sky</u>. Traveling by <u>airplane</u> is my favorite way to travel because <u>I like to get where I'm going fast</u>.

# Answer Key

Sample response 2
I prefer to travel by <u>train or boat</u>. I like traveling by <u>train or boat</u> because <u>it is inexpensive. It is easier because I don't have to make the effort to go out to the airport.</u> I like to travel by <u>train or boat</u> because <u>I despise flying.</u> In addition, I like <u>to enjoy the scenery that is located near the train route.</u> Traveling by <u>train or boat</u> is my favorite way to travel because <u>it requires the least effort.</u>

## Integrated

### Page 125
**B**
1. The students are discussing <u>which classes to take next semester.</u>
2. The student <u>can't decide if he should take a full course load or not.</u>
3. The student <u>should take a full course load so that he finishes sooner.</u>

### Page 126
**A**

| Man | Woman |
|---|---|
| • Choosing <u>courses</u> <br> • Can't decide if <u>he should take a full course load</u> <br> • Maybe <u>join extra-curricular activity</u> <br> • A sports club or <u>drama club</u> <br> • And could start <u>working sooner</u> <br> • And could earn <u>money</u> <br> • This is a <u>difficult decision</u> | • That would be <u>fun</u> <br> • What kind of <u>club would you join</u>? <br> • If more courses, could <u>finish degree faster</u> <br> • Money is not so <u>important</u> <br> • If join a club then can <u>have different experiences</u> and meet <u>lots of new people</u> |

**B**
1. The students discuss <u>finishing his degree faster and being able to start work and begin earning money.</u>
2. The students discuss <u>having different experiences and meeting new people.</u>

### Page 127
**D**

The conversation is about <u>how many classes the man should take.</u>
A. Take fewer classes and <u>do extra-curricular activity</u>
  1. Join a <u>sports club</u>
  2. Do <u>volunteer work</u>
B. Take many courses
  1. finish <u>degree faster</u>
  2. start working and <u>earning money</u>
C. Join a club and <u>have more fun</u>
  1. Have <u>interesting experiences</u>
  2. Meet <u>new people</u>

Conclusion: I think <u>he should join a club because studying is not the only important thing.</u>

**E**

Conclusion: I think he should <u>take a full course load</u> because <u>university is for studying and he should be a serious student to prepare for his future.</u>

**G**
1. audition    2. course load   3. extra-curricular
4. degree      5. On the other hand

### Page 128
**Step 1**

| Man | Woman |
|---|---|
| • Auditions for the <u>school play</u> <br> • You should <u>audition</u> <br> • It would be <u>fun</u> <br> • It would be <u>good experience</u> <br> • If you join the play you won't <u>have time to spend with your friends</u> | • I want to but <u>I don't know if I have time</u> <br> • I have to <u>study for final exams</u> <br> • Final exams <u>are coming and I want good grades</u> <br> • If I don't do well my parents will be <u>disappointed</u> <br> • But they also like to <u>watch me act</u> <br> • I don't know <u>what to do</u> |

**Step 3**

The conversation is about <u>joining the school play.</u>
A. Wants to join the play because
  1. <u>Fun</u>
  2. Good <u>experience</u>
  3. Parents enjoy <u>watching</u>
B. Thinks she should study because
  1. Get <u>good grades</u>
  2. Don't <u>disappoint parents</u>
  3. Can spend time <u>with friends</u>
Conclusion: I would prefer <u>to join the school play because it would be more fun.</u>

### Page 129
**Step 4**

The conversation is about <u>joining the school play.</u> The female student wants to <u>appear in the play</u> because <u>it would be fun and a good experience. Also, her parents enjoy watching her in plays.</u> However, she thinks <u>she should study</u> because <u>she wants to get good grades and she doesn't want to disappoint her parents. She would also have more time to spend with friends.</u>

I would prefer <u>to join the school play</u> because <u>it would be more fun and a great experience.</u>

<u>I would prefer to study for final exams</u> because <u>it's important to get good grades on exams.</u>

## Page 130

1. hectic
2. appearing
3. despise
4. late
5. disappoint
6. earn

# [ Unit 12 ]

**Independent**

## Page 131

**B**

1. I like to <u>play online games</u>.
2. I spend <u>about an hour every day</u> on the Internet.
3. I use the Internet <u>after school</u>.

## Page 132

**A**

1. My favorite website is ESPN.com.
2. It is my favorite website because I love to read about sports.
3. I trust the website because the writers are all smart.
4. I think it's a good website because it has a lot of good writing and a lot of excellent features.

**B**

| | |
|---|---|
| Resource | Research |
| Interactive | Information |
| World Wide Web | Menu |
| Hyperlink | |

**C**

I usually have to do research for <u>my history classes</u>.
I usually <u>read my old text books</u> to get information.
It usually takes <u>about 20 minutes</u> to find the information I need.
I use <u>my books</u> because <u>I trust the information and they are next to my desk</u>.

**D**

| | |
|---|---|
| Library | Look up |
| Efficient | Know how to do it |
| Trusted | Source |
| Find | |

## Page 133

**F**

Sample response 1

Good place for research

**First reason:**
Efficient

**Second reason:**
More information than even the biggest library

**Think this because:**
Rapidly answer questions
So much information

**Think that:** The Internet is a good place for research. It is vast and fast.

Sample response 2

Not a good place for research.

**First reason:**
Hard to control

**Second reason:**
Hard to find information

**Think this because:**
Anyone can write what they want
Not reliable

**Think that:** The Internet is great but isn't always good for research.

**G**

1. source
2. Professional
3. data
4. vast
5. topic

## Page 134

**Step 2**

Sample response 1

Internet is great for gathering information

**First reason:**
Information on almost any topic

**Second reason:**
Often from professional sources

**Think this because:**
Information for research or entertainment
Vast amount of information

**Think that:** Internet is good for research

Sample response 2

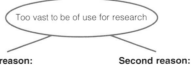

Too vast to be of use for research

**First reason:**
Huge amount of data from unprofessional sources

**Second reason:**
Can get lost

**Think this because:**
Unreliable data
Too much data

**Think that:** Internet is bad for research

# Answer Key

## Step 3
**Sample response 1**
I think the Internet is <u>a great place for gathering information</u>. The Internet is <u>so vast and has so much data that you can find information on almost any topic</u>. People can <u>use the Internet for research or for entertainment</u>. The information on the Internet is <u>often from professional sources</u>. The Internet is good for research because <u>you can rapidly find a vast amount of information</u>.

**Sample response 2**
I think the Internet is <u>too vast to be of any real use for research</u>. The Internet is <u>full of a huge amount of data that isn't from professional sources</u>. People can <u>get lost in the rapidly moving mass of data</u>. The information on the Internet is <u>too unreliable to be of any real use</u>. The Internet is bad for research because <u>there is too much unreliable information</u>.

## Integrated

### Page 135
**B**
1. The lecture is about <u>orchestras</u>.
2. An orchestra has <u>four sections</u>.
3. I think the professor will talk about <u>what the different sections in an orchestra do.</u>

### Page 136
**A**
- Group who plays <u>music is called an orchestra</u>
- Full-size is about one <u>hundred players</u>
- All play different <u>instruments</u>
- Has many groups called <u>sections</u>
- There are four <u>big sections</u>
- Instruments made of wood, <u>brass, drums, and string</u>
- Orchestra leader is called the <u>conductor</u>
- Uses small stick, called a <u>baton</u>
- Players watch it to see how <u>fast or slowly they should play</u>

**B**
1. The four sections of an orchestra are <u>wood, brass, drum, and violin (or string)</u>.
2. The conductor leads the orchestra with a <u>baton</u> that shows players <u>how quickly or slowly</u> they should play.

### Page 137
**D**
The lecture is about <u>orchestras</u>.
A. The one hundred players
  1. make <u>beautiful music</u>
  2. play <u>different instruments</u>
B. Orchestra sections
  1. <u>Wood</u>
  2. <u>Brass</u>
  3. <u>Drums</u>
  4. <u>String (violin)</u>
C. The Orchestra leader
  1. is called <u>a conductor</u>
  2. knows <u>the music well</u>
  3. knows <u>what the players have to do</u>
  4. uses a small stick called <u>a baton to show how quickly to play</u>

**F**
1. stretch   2. orchestra  3. full-sized
4. group     5. hollow

### Page 138
**Step 1**
- String section is <u>biggest group in orchestra</u>
- String instruments are violins, <u>violas</u>, cellos, double basses, and <u>pianos</u>
- Instruments made of <u>wood are hollow inside</u>
- Strings are made of <u>steel</u> or nylon and <u>stretched over holes</u>
- Players pull long sticks called <u>bows</u>
- Bows are made of <u>horsehair</u>
- The piano is a <u>string instrument</u>
- It has small strings and <u>hammers inside it</u>
- Sound is made when a hammer hits a <u>string</u>

**Step 3**
The lecture is about <u>stringed instruments, the biggest section in the orchestra</u>.
A. String instruments
  1. Violin
  2. Viola
  3. Cello
  4. Double bass
  5. Piano
B. They
  1. are made of wood
  2. are hollow <u>inside</u>
  3. have strings of steel or <u>nylon</u>
C. Sound is made with a bow pulled <u>over strings</u>
D. Piano
  1. has <u>strings and hammers</u>
  2. hammers hit <u>strings</u>

## Page 139

### Step 4

The lecture is about <u>string instruments</u>. The five string instruments are <u>violin, viola, cello, double bass and the piano</u>. They are made of <u>wood. They are hollow and have strings made of steel and nylon</u>. Sound is made <u>when a bow made of horsehair is pulled across the strings</u>. A piano is also a string instrument. Sound is made when <u>the small hammer in the piano hits a small string</u>.

### Page 140

1. brass
2. conductor
3. Excess
4. rapidly
5. baton
6. efficient

# [ Review 2 ]

## Independent 1

### Page 141

### Step 2

Sample response 1

Celebrate birthday at home

**First reason:**
Less expensive

**Second reason:**
Don't have to make arrangements

**Like to:**
Watch a movie
Share a meal

**I prefer:** To celebrate at home with friends

Sample response 2

Celebrate at a restaurant

**First reason:**
Less clean-up

**Second reason:**
Share conversation over a meal

**Like to:**
Be out with friends

**I prefer:** Celebrating at restaurants

### Step 3

Sample response 1

I think it is best to celebrate a birthday <u>by staying home</u>. I would like to celebrate my birthday by <u>having a group of my friends come to my house and share a meal. In addition, it would be fun to have some sort of entertainment like watching a movie</u>. I think this is the best way to celebrate <u>because I don't have to make plans at a restaurant and it is less expensive</u>.

Sample response 2

I think it is best to celebrate a birthday <u>by going to a restaurant</u>. I would like to celebrate my birthday by <u>having a group of my friends share a meal and conversation with me at a restaurant</u>. I think this is the best way to celebrate because <u>I don't have to clean up a mess and I get to be with my friends over a meal</u>.

## Integrated 1

### Page 142

### Step 2

Deserts
- There are <u>four major types of deserts</u>
- They have very little <u>water</u>
- Animals' main water sources are <u>things like seeds and roots</u>

Forests
- There are <u>three different types of forests</u>
- They have a lot of water <u>sources</u>
- They are usually <u>damp and have cool air</u>

Forests and deserts
- A lot more plants and animals <u>live in the forest</u>
- There is more water in the <u>forest</u>

### Page 143

### Step 4

The passage and the lecture are about <u>deserts and forests</u>

A. Deserts
  1. There are <u>four different types of deserts</u>
  2. The largest one is <u>the Sahara desert</u>
  3. Animals need little <u>water to survive</u>

B. Forests
  1. The largest rainforest is the <u>Amazon Jungle</u>
  2. Forests <u>are being cut down</u>
  3. There are <u>a lot more plants and animals</u>
  4. There is more <u>water</u>

### Step 5

The passage and lecture were about <u>deserts and forests</u>. There are <u>four different types</u> of deserts. The largest desert is <u>the Sahara Desert</u>. Animals need little <u>water to survive</u> in the desert. The largest rainforest is the <u>Amazon Jungle</u>. Many rainforests are being <u>cut down</u>. However, there are <u>a lot more plants and animals in the forest</u> because <u>there is more water</u>.

# Answer Key

## Integrated 2

### Page 144

### Step 1

| Female student | Male student |
|---|---|
| • Ready for <u>school to start</u><br>• Options?<br>• Why take only <u>a few?</u><br>• Take a few then get <u>a job to make money and relax</u> | • Needs to choose <u>classes</u><br>• Take a lot of classes or <u>a few classes</u><br>• Take a few classes then can <u>get a job as well</u><br>• Take many classes then can <u>finish school quicker</u><br>• Wants to take art and <u>math classes</u><br>• Could finish school <u>this year</u><br>• Doesn't know <u>what to do</u> |

### Step 3

The conversation is about <u>a student deciding how many classes he should take</u>.
A. The student must choose whether <u>to take a lot of easy classes or a few hard classes</u>
B. Take a lot of classes
  1. Can finish <u>school this year</u>
  2. Can take classes he <u>really wants</u>
C. Take a few classes
  1. Can get <u>a job</u>
  2. Make <u>money</u>
  3. <u>Relax</u>
Conclusion: I would prefer <u>to take a few classes and earn money because he could use it to pay for school. There will always be art and math classes he can take</u>.

Conclusion: I would prefer <u>to take more classes and finish school sooner. Plus it would be a shame not to take the classes he really wants</u>.

### Page 145

### Step 4

Example 1
The conversation is about <u>a student deciding how many classes he should take</u>. The student must choose <u>whether to take a lot of easy classes or a few hard classes</u>. If he takes a lot of <u>classes, then he can finish school this year. He could also take the classes he really wants</u>. If he only takes <u>a few classes, then he can get a job and make money. He could also relax</u>.

I would prefer <u>to take a few classes and earn money because he could use it to pay for school. There will always be art and math classes he can take</u>.

I would prefer <u>to take more classes and finish school next year. Plus it would be a shame not to take the classes he really wants</u>.

## Independent 2

### Page 146

### Step 2

Sample response 1

**First reason:** Helps decide what is of interest
**Second reason:** Learn a lot of different things
**Better because:** Helps decide what subject to study later in school
**Think that:** Better to take many different courses

Sample response 1

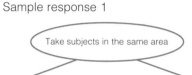

**First reason:** Easier to focus on one subject
**Second reason:** Better to take closely related courses
**Better because:** Usually a subject that is of interest
**I think that:** Better to take subjects in one area

### Step 3

Sample response 1
I think students should <u>take a course load with a vast array of subjects to figure out what interests them</u>. Students usually find it <u>more enjoyable to take a course load with different subjects</u> because <u>it gives them a chance to learn different things and decide what subject they would like to learn more of later on in school</u>. I think it is better to <u>take a vast array of courses</u> because <u>it is a good way to find the subjects that interest you</u>.

Sample response 2
I think students should <u>take a course load that is mainly in one subject</u>. Students usually find it <u>easier to focus on one subject</u> because <u>it is easier to think about just one thing opposed to many different things, especially if the subject is of interest to them</u>. I think it is better to <u>take courses all from one area</u> because <u>it is easier to focus on only one area of study</u>.